DviH

TRANSFERRING LEARNING
TO BEHAVIOR

TRANSFERRING LEARNING TO BEHAVIOR

Using the Four Levels to Improve Performance

DONALD L. KIRKPATRICK, PhD
AND
JAMES D. KIRKPATRICK, PhD

BERRETT-KOEHLER PUBLISHERS, INC.
San Francisco

Berrett-Koehler Publishers, Inc.
235 Montgomery Street, Suite 650
San Francisco, CA 94104-2916
Tel: (415) 288-0260   Fax: (415) 362-2512   www.bkconnection.com

ORDERING INFORMATION

Quantity sales. Special discounts are available on quantity purchases by corporations,
associations, and others. For details, contact the "Special Sales Department" at the Berrett-
Koehler address above.

Individual sales. Berrett-Koehler publications are available through most bookstores.
They can also be ordered directly from Berrett-Koehler: Tel: (800) 929-2929; Fax: (802)
864-7626; www.bkconnection.com

Orders for college textbook/course adoption use. Please contact Berrett-Koehler: Tel:
(800) 929-2929; Fax: (802) 864-7626.

Orders by U.S. trade bookstores and wholesalers. Please contact Ingram Publisher Services,
Tel: (800) 509-4887; Fax: (800) 838-1149; E-mail: customer.service@ingrampublisherservices
.com; or visit www.ingrampublisherservices.com/Ordering for details about electronic ordering.

Berrett-Koehler and the BK logo are registered trademarks of Berrett-Koehler Publishers, Inc.

Printed in the United States of America
Berrett-Koehler books are printed on long-lasting acid-free paper. When it is available, we
choose paper that has been manufactured by environmentally responsible processes. These
may include using trees grown in sustainable forests, incorporating recycled paper,
minimizing chlorine in bleaching, or recycling the energy produced at the paper mill.

Library of Congress Cataloging-in-Publication Data

Kirkpatrick, Donald L.
　　　　Transferring learning to behavior : using the four levels to improve performance / by
　　Donald L. Kirkpatrick and James D. Kirkpatrick.
　　　　　p.　cm.
　　Includes bibliographical references and index.
　　ISBN: 978-1-57675-325-5
　　1. Employees—Training of.　2. Performance technology.　3. Organizational learning.　4.
　　Organizational behavior.　I. Kirkpatrick, James D., 1952-　II. Title.
　　HF5549.5.T7K572 2005
　　658.3'124—dc22　　　　　　　　　　　　　　　　　　　　　　　2004062370

First Edition
14　　13　　12　　11　　10　　　　　　　　10　9　8　7　6　5　4　3

Contents

Foreword

During much of the past century, training programs tended to fall into two camps: classroom instruction, which focused mainly on imparting knowledge, and on-the-job training, where the emphasis was on imparting skills. The former stressed the concepts, principles, rules, and procedures to be learned and evaluated in class. The latter stressed the behaviors to be displayed and evaluated in the workplace.

More recently trainers and consultants have realized that their job is not primarily to impart information but rather to improve performance by changing behavior. And that's the focus of this book.

Unlike the majority of books that are written primarily for training specialists and Human Resource managers, this book is chock full of helpful hints for anyone who is responsible for the performance of others, from group leaders and technical support people to owners of small businesses and supervisors, managers, and, yes, corporate executives.

Hats off to the Kirkpatricks, Don and Jim, father and son. As Vice President of First Indiana Bank's Corporate University, Jim is in the enviable position to implement a highly successful performance improvement program. Jim uses the Kirkpatrick four-level model of evaluation developed by Dad a half-century ago as the foundation (are we not surprised). He has then drawn on two well-established models and illustrates them with lucid examples of each:

- the Balanced Scorecard approach by Kaplan and Norton, balancing support and accountability
- the Kouzes-Posner leadership model and its five dimensions

Throughout the book Jim manages to regale us with colorful anecdotes and analogies that dramatize his learning points. For example, we recognize his utter failure in attempting to teach his wife how to fish and play golf, his two main pastimes. We rejoice in her success as a registered nurse in keeping Jim's dad alive following a heart stoppage. We admire her ability to motivate Jim to move the piano after repeated requests had failed.

Nuggets of advice are scattered throughout the book, clustered around these predominant themes:

- Performance improvement requires behavior change.
- A learning culture is necessary to support and sustain behavior change.
- The organization must deal with all types of trainees: reachers, responders, and resisters.
- A balanced scorecard approach can be used to affix accountability, track performance, and recognize achievement.

In the introductory chapter, Don summarizes the relevance of four-level evaluations in the twenty-first century, stressing that course design and development should begin with Level 4—What measurable results do I want?—and work backward from there, through Levels 3, 2, and 1.

The remaining pages divide into two halves: a detailed look at Jim's program at First Indiana Bank (Chapters 1–8) and a collection of ten case studies that illustrate the concepts and procedures discussed earlier (Chapters 9–10).

Fortunately, Jim is blessed with the same finely honed sense of humor that I've come to enjoy from his dad. Moreover, the joke is usually at Jim's expense, never at another's. It's refreshing to find Human Resource Department books that are entertaining as well as helpful. I am pleased to recommend this book . . . for your enjoyment and your learning.

Scott B. Parry, PhD

Preface

From Don:

For many years, I have given presentations and conducted workshops on my four levels for evaluating training programs. The content has been basically the same.

Within the last five years, my son, Dr. James Kirkpatrick, has been applying the levels in his organization, First Indiana Bank, where he is the Vice President of First Indiana's Corporate University. Jim is responsible for all training and development activities as well as the application of the training to improve results. He has given many presentations and conducted workshops in the United States and abroad. His main subjects are the application of the four levels, the transfer of learning to on-the-job behavior, and linking training to strategy using balanced scorecards.

The transfer of training is a major challenge facing training professionals. Jim has asked me to work with him to write a practical book incorporating my four levels into the application. Then Steve Piersanti, president of Berrett-Koehler Publishers Inc., agreed to publish this book.

Jim challenged me to write Chapter 1, "The Four Levels in the twenty-first century." His first question was, "How much has your approach changed since you introduced the four levels in 1959 in a series of articles in the *T&D*, the publication of the American Society for Training and Development (ASTD)"?

So, I wrote Chapter 1 to provide the background for the rest of the book, which Jim wrote. We hope it will help you understand and apply the four levels, and provide practical suggestions for transferring learning into effective behavior.

Donald L. Kirkpatrick

From Jim:

I had conducted seminars with my father, Don Kirkpatrick, for the University of Wisconsin Management Institute for several years, but to be honest, had not paid all that much attention to his famous four levels. That all changed in 1998. A friend and colleague of mine, John Galloway, was finishing a master's degree at Indiana University/Purdue University at Indianapolis and heard that my father was coming to Indianapolis to visit my family and me. "Jim, do you think you could get your father to meet with my class for a dinner talk?" I said I thought so, and quickly arranged it. John invited me, so I sat in on dad's presentation on *Evaluating Training Programs*. Naturally he focused on the four levels. Much to my embarrassment, I was not even sure what they were: Reaction, Learning, Behavior, and Results. I knew they began with reaction and ended with results, but was a bit confused about the middle two.

I listened intently to that 45-minute talk and even took notes. I remember being impressed by two things. One was how simple and practical the four levels were. The other was how impressed his audience was with him and his presentation. I had been a psychologist for a number of years, a career consultant, and a management consultant, but for some reason hadn't found it necessary to weave the four levels into my work.

I drove him to my house that night and asked him some followup questions on the way. As I was asking and he was answering, I started to piece together the beginnings of a plan to integrate his four levels into my work. I had begun working for First Indiana Bank in Indianapolis, Indiana, the previous year. First Indiana is an independent, community bank of about 800 employees (we call them "associates") that has since made a successful transition from a thrift to a national bank. In the six years since then, I have applied the four levels in many different ways at First Indiana.

I am currently the Director of First Indiana Bank's Corporate University. My major responsibilities include our balanced scorecard management system, leadership development, associate and career development, training, process improvement, and recognition. I do find time and the need, however, to attend conferences on training and development, and frequently get to conduct workshops at those conferences, often with my father. The idea and material for this book comes from my work, those conferences and workshops, and most importantly, from Don.

The purpose of this book is twofold. First, it operationalizes Don's book, *Evaluating Training Programs: The Four Levels* (second ed., Berrett-Koehler, 1998). It not only offers new ideas regarding evaluation, but utilizes the model in effectively implementing strategy by specifically linking and aligning training to strategy. Second, it uses the four levels as the foundation to attacking the specific challenge of transferring learning (Level 2) to behavior (Level 3). According to many training executives and trainers across the globe, this remains one of the top training challenges in organizations of all sorts. Specifically, it explains the challenge, then offers solutions from the authors as well as from professionals in varying kinds of organizations.

This book is outlined into four parts. Part One identifies and assesses the challenge of transferring learning to behavior. It begins with an overview of the four levels to set the foundation, reviews their use in the twenty-first century, then discusses the specific challenge. Of particular importance is the increasing pressure from senior executives and boards on training departments and corporate universities to demonstrate the bottom-line results that come from training. This pressure, along with economical challenges and technological opportunities, has forced us to view training from a new perspective. There is a worldwide movement toward converting training departments to corporate universities, and corporate trainers to internal business consultants. This offers not only challenges but also opportunities, thus expanding the role and importance of the four levels. Even with things changing so fast, the eons-old fact still exists that individuals and groups are more comfortable staying the same than changing. Thus, our challenge and this book.

Part Two details five foundations for success. It would be unfair and misleading to skip this part of the book and just move to specific solutions to transferring learning to behavior. I learned this lesson the hard way. In 1997, I was directed to lead First Indiana Bank into the world of Total Quality Management (TQM). I eagerly accepted the challenge and took over the leadership of our Total Quality Council and quickly developed corporate-wide courses in TQM. The principles of TQM are sound. My efforts were sincere. Hundreds of associates learned how to flowchart their work processes, set standards, and develop work flow improvement action plans. They were equally sincere in making it all work. Unfortunately, after months of hard work, it didn't "stick." Learning TQM principles and methods did not transfer to new behaviors and positive results. Several of the foundations for success were not present. The specific foundations presented are: a Strategic Focus, an Effective Change Management Model, the Right Kind of Leadership, an Effective Measurement System, and Success with Levels 1 and 2. You'll have to read into those chapters to discover just which ones were lacking that doomed our TQM implementation.

Part Three attacks the challenge. The basic premise is that two significant forces have to be balanced for this successful transfer, support and accountability. Examples of both are provided, along with a chapter entitled "The Glue to Hold It Together," which addresses feedback, coaching, and other followup methods to ensure success.

Finally, Part Four offers case studies from successful corporations and training leaders. They reveal foundational reasons for their success as well as specific best practices. A variety of types of organizations were selected, as was a great variance in scope, from the large corporation to the individual practicing trainer.

I wish to thank my wife, Denise, and my parents, Don and Fern Kirkpatrick, for their encouragement and guidance with the ideas in this book. I also want to thank Marni, Nancy, Marianne, and Tracy from First Indiana for modeling the way of great leadership and training practices; Sharon Spencer at First Indiana for her technical assistance with scorecards and graphs (only on her lunch hour!); friends and colleagues Dale Sears and John Galloway for their encouragement and significant text contributions; Scott Parry for the glowing foreword; the many reviewers and distinguished colleagues who offered kind words of suggestion and endorsement; and Steve Piersanti, President of Berrett-Koehler Publishers, for his continuous support and guidance.

Finally, I am grateful to the training leaders who provided best prac-

tice case studies that reflect their commitment to the field, training expertise, and generosity in sharing it with the rest of us.

James D. Kirkpatrick

Note: Obviously more challenges to improving performance exist
than can be covered in one book. Therefore, we will soon be com-
mencing the second in this series of attacking training and performance challenges. While the exact title is not yet set, it will focus on
Level 4—generating, measuring, evaluating, and communicating results. We know that you—our professional colleagues—use a variety of
methods to successfully meet the challenges of Level 4. We want this
upcoming book to include what you as practitioners and consultants
have found to be effective. Please e-mail us stories, cases, examples,
methods, and tools that you have worked for you. One of us will get
back to you and see if what you offer might offer a significant contribution to our book. Send your information to Jim at jim.kirkpatrick@
insightbb.com.

PART I

THE FOUR LEVELS'
BIGGEST CHALLENGE

Part One begins with Chapter 1, written by Don, as an overview of the Four Levels of Evaluating Training Programs—*Reaction, Learning, Behavior*, and *Results*. He covers the history of their development and how they are being applied today.

Chapter Two attacks the challenge—How can we as trainers and training managers carry forth the good training we offer employees to new behaviors and subsequent results? This challenge, of course, is huge, since we lose much of our influence as trainees return to their jobs. In other words, Levels 1 and 2 are within our control; Levels 3 and 4 are only within our influence.

Included in these chapters and throughout the book are case examples and best practices from Jim's own work and that of his colleagues. Many readers will be able to apply effectively the principles and methods outlined in Parts Two and Three. Others will benefit more from reading about real-life challenges and subsequent best practices in Part Four. Thus, the book is a balance of both.

Chapter 1

The Four Levels in the 21st Century

In 1954, at the University of Wisconsin in Madison, I (Don) completed my PhD dissertation entitled "Evaluating a Human Relations Training Program for Supervisors." Based on the dissertation, I wrote a series of four articles for the *T&D* of the American Society for Training and Development (ASTD): "Evaluating Reaction," "Evaluating Learning," "Evaluating Behavior," and "Evaluating Results."

At that time, training professionals were struggling with the word "evaluation." There was no common language and no easy way to communicate what "evaluation" meant and how to accomplish it. Trainers began to accept my four levels and passed the word to others. Soon, it came to be called the "Kirkpatrick Model." The concepts, principles, and techniques were communicated from one professional to another as trainers began to apply one or more of the levels.

In 1993, a training friend, Jane Holcomb, told me that trainers were talking about the four levels but couldn't find the articles that had been written in 1959. She said, "Write a book!" So I decided to do it.

I realized trainers want to know more than the concepts, principles, and techniques. They want to know what other professionals were doing to apply them. So I wrote the book in two parts. Part One contains a description of the levels, guidelines for each, and suggested forms and approaches. Part Two contains case studies of organizations that had applied one or more of the levels.

My first contact for a case study was Dave Basarab, who was responsible for evaluating training programs at Motorola. When I told him who I was, he replied, "Don Kirkpatrick? We use your four levels all over the world!" He was willing to write a case study and write the introduction to the book. He suggested my contacting Arthur Andersen and Intel for additional case studies. They were willing and suggested others. The first edition was published in 1994 and the second in 1998 with case studies from Motorola, Intel, Cisco, The Gap, First Union National Bank, Kemper Insurance, Duke Energy, the City of Los Angeles, St. Luke's Hospital, and the University of Wisconsin's Management Institute. The book has been a best seller and has been translated into Spanish, Polish, and Turkish.

My son Jim asked me, "How has your model changed since it was introduced in 1959?" I told him the model remains essentially the same. The concepts, principles, and techniques are as applicable today as they were when the model was first introduced. I am still getting requests from universities and professional and private organizations to present the four levels in keynote addresses at their conferences.

I have yet to receive a comment that they are out of date. The one major modification—or rather, addition—is Return on Investment or ROI that author and consultant Jack Phillips has called Level 5, separating it from Level 4. Even for those who agree with Phillips' thinking, my levels continue to be the basis for evaluation around the world.

At the 2004 national conference of ASTD, I was given the award for Lifetime Achievement in Workplace Learning and Performance to "recognize an individual for a body of work that has had significant impact on the field of workplace learning and performance." In announcing the award, ASTD stated, "Spare and elegant, the Kirkpatrick model has been the most widely used evaluation method for more than forty years. His plan is to continue communicating the four levels, and there is, no doubt, a new audience waiting to hear."

Here is a brief description of the four levels and the guidelines I have suggested.

Level 1: Reaction

How do trainees react to the program, or better, what is the measure of customer satisfaction? Whether they attend a program where they have to pay a fee or attend an in-house program where only time is required, they are "customers." Their reaction is important. In a situation where they pay, their reaction determines whether they attend again or recommend the training to others from their organization. Universities, professional organizations, and consultants who conduct these kinds of programs should be very interested in the reaction of participants. In an in-house situation, comments to others when participants return to their jobs have a major impact on future training programs and budgets.

Reactions of participants should be measured on all programs for two reasons: to let the participants know that trainers value their reactions, and to measure their reactions and obtain suggestions for improvement.

Guidelines for Evaluating Reaction

1. Determine what you want to find out.
2. Design a form that will quantify reactions.
3. Encourage written comments.
4. Get 100 percent immediate response.
5. Develop an acceptable standard.
6. Measure reactions against the standard.

Level 2: Learning

To what extent has learning occurred? Three things can be accomplished in a training program:

1. Understand the concepts, principles, and techniques being taught.
2. Develop and/or improve skills.
3. Change attitudes.

All programs have the objective of increasing the knowledge of the participants. Some programs also have the objective of increasing the technical or sales skills of the participants. And some programs, such as "Diversity Training," are aimed at changing attitudes.

Learning evaluations should be targeted to the specific objectives of the program and should be used to evaluate all programs.

Guidelines for Evaluating Learning

1. Measure knowledge, skill, and/or attitudes before and after the training.
2. Use a paper-and-pencil test for knowledge and attitudes.
3. Use a performance test for skills.
4. Get 100 percent response.
5. If practical, use a control group that does not receive the training to compare with the experimental group that receives the training.

Level 3: Behavior

To what extent has on-the-job behavior changed as a result of the program? This is the most difficult to measure and probably the most important. If the trainees do not apply what they learned, the program has been a failure even if learning has taken place. Therefore, measuring behavior change is necessary, not only to see if behavior has changed, but also to determine the reasons why change has not occurred.

It would be an almost impossible task to evaluate all programs in terms of change in behavior. Therefore, a sampling approach should be used.

Guidelines for Evaluating Behavior

1. If possible, evaluate on before and after training. It is usually impossible to do this, so it becomes necessary to do it after the program and determine what the participant is doing differently than he/she was doing before the program.
2. Allow time for the behavior to change.
3. Survey and/or interview one or more of the following:

    a. The trainee
    b. The bosses of the trainee

    c. The subordinates of the trainee

    d. Others who observe the behavior of the trainee

4. Get 100 percent response or a sampling.

5. Repeat at appropriate times.

6. Use a control group if practical.

7. Consider the cost of the evaluation versus the possible benefits.

Level 4: Results

To what extent have results occurred because of the training? Results could be determined by many factors including less turnover, improved quantity of work, improved quality, reduction of waste, reduction in wasted time, increased sales, reduction in costs, increase in profits, and return on investment (ROI).

As in the case of evaluating behavior, evaluation should be done only on those programs considered most important or most expensive. It has been recommended that ROI should only be attempted on about 5 percent of an organization's programs.

Guidelines for Evaluating Results

1. Measure on before and after training.

2. Allow time for possible results to take place.

3. Repeat at appropriate times.

4. Use a control group if practical.

5. Consider the cost of the evaluation versus the possible benefits.

THE CHANGING ROLE OF TRAINING

This is a changing world we live in. *T&D*, American Society for Training and Development's monthly magazine, frequently discusses the changing trends in our industry. In the May 2004 issue, it notes, "During the past decade, workplace learning and performance professionals have faced corporate demands, economic uncertainly, and personal needs and dilemmas that have significantly affected their tasks and role. Trainers are now referred to as performance analysts. Instead of working full-time in large corporations, many have joined consulting organizations that outsource expertise. Instead of working in traditional roles of instructors, mentors, or coaches, they assist managers to become instructors, mentors, or coaches with their employees" (p. 48). The December 2003 issue is titled, "The Future of the Profession Formerly Known as Training." The articles basically talk about recent, rather drastic changes in the field of training. We've reached the point where many professionals don't even like to use the term *training* anymore. Corporate Universities are springing up all over the world. A friend and colleague of ours, Annick Renaud-Coulon, has organized a thriving Corporate University Club in Europe; Karen Barley, president of Corporate University Enterprise, has found the same in this country. This trend and the reasons behind it have led many companies to transition from a training department to a Corporate University.

Specifically, they tend to focus on two major aspects—comprehensive, cross-functional programs of study and a business consulting model. The programs of study ensure that employees at different levels and in different job groups get the exact training they need, as opposed to a hit-and-miss approach. The business consulting model allows for linking training with line-of-business needs. Together, they reinforce the pressure we all feel to improve the efficiency and effectiveness of training.

CURRENT APPLICATIONS OF THE FOUR LEVELS

Even though I wrote my series of articles that gave birth to the four levels in 1959, their obvious use in evaluating training effectiveness remains relevant and vibrant today. The four levels serve more than the obvious purpose of evaluating training after the fact; they are a great model for developing programs.

I would like to point out a small notation in my book, *Evaluating Training Programs: The Four Levels*. In the last paragraph on page 14, I state, ". . . to ensure the effectiveness of a training program, time and emphasis should be put on the planning and implementation of the program." In other words, start with the end in mind. I know this to be a very common use of the four levels today.

The business consulting model for training is relevant here. Many training departments within organizations offer a variety of courses, from Time Management to Teambuilding to Sales Effectiveness, never being sure the courses actually align with an identified business need. Most savvy training leaders have a different approach. Instead of developing a training program or coaching intervention based on what they *think* the need is, they conduct a needs assessment with the line-of-business leader in which they focus on the need, problem, or opportunity. This, of course, acts to align the new training with the actual business need.

Here is where the four levels enter the picture. Start with Level 4 (results) and determine with the line-of-business managers what needs to happen. Then, work backward with the question, "What behaviors (Level 3) need to be put into practice to achieve the desired results?" Then, ask, "What knowledge, skills, and attitudes (Level 2) will the targeted employees need to have to behave appropriately?" Follow by, "How will we get them to come to training and be receptive to these changes (Level 1)?"

Besides utilizing the four levels before and after training, they also come in handy *during* training. When I am conducting a workshop on the four levels, I regularly ask myself, "Are they with me? What can I do to improve their receptiveness and attention (Level 1)?" I also use methods to determine how well they are catching what I am pitching (Level 2). And I surely spend time in all my training to find out how participants plan to implement (Level 3) what they are learning, and how they will measure results (Level 4).

FINAL THOUGHTS

Don't let the challenge of evaluating training overwhelm you. Many trainers I know start out with evaluating Level 1 until they are comfortable with it. Then they move on to Level 2 until they feel good about that, then on to Level 3 and Level 4. Also keep in mind that you don't have to get it perfect the first time through, and that using a sample of your trainee population can be very effective.

Chapter 2

_____

The Challenge: Transferring Learning to Behavior

I (Jim) began working for First Indiana Bank in 1997 after several years as a management and career consultant. My boss is Marni McKinney, Chairman of First Indiana Bank and CEO of First Indiana Corporation. When I first started, she told me, "Jim, when you plan and conduct training, please make sure that participants find it worthwhile and want to come back for more."

In 1998 she asked me, "How do you think our training is going? I surely hope people are not only enjoying it, but are learning something!" And in 2000 she said, "You know, our people are spending a lot of time in training. I would really like to know if they are able to apply what they are learning."

Two years ago (2002), she said, "As you know, we have great responsibility to our shareholders to meet our financial goals for 2003 and beyond. I need to be able to see how training is impacting the bottom line. I don't want people spending a lot of time away from their jobs in activities that are not directly contributing to positive results."

Each time, we engaged in interesting, fruitful discussion. I modified training accordingly, to the wishes of my boss. Each time, however, the challenge became greater. The challenges in 1997 and 1998 were moderate—make training interesting, and make sure people are learning relevant skills and methods. The challenges in 2000, and certainly 2002, were much more substantial. How could I do what she asked and be able to *demonstrate* it? After all, once our trainees leave the classroom, I and my direct reports lose control and can only rely on our influencing skills.

Marni found her own way through the four levels by observing from her role as chairman and by participating in training throughout those years. The path she took is by no means uncommon. For one thing, the economy has been tight since late 1990s, and 9/11 only made things worse. Competition remains fierce. Executives are looking everywhere for opportunities to generate income and cut costs. With that goes the need to increase training effectiveness and efficiency. Managers are reluctant to release their direct reports to all-day training programs. Will their people make up for "lost time" by improving their effectiveness as a result of training? Many of our managers want training to be shorter and/or to be conducted over the lunch hour. Along with this comes the need for training managers to justify in-house training and for consultants to demonstrate that their services are worthwhile and cost-effective. Effective implementation of the four levels certainly helps when we must decide which programs to continue, which to modify, and which to eliminate.

I believe that the best way to introduce the specific challenge of transferring learning to behavior is with an illustration. After our Total Quality Management fiasco (don't worry, I'll get to it in the next chapter), First Indiana Bank came to the realization that we needed a stronger scientific approach to our business and even thought TQM could have provided that for us if we had implemented it correctly. In 1998, we decided that Kaplan and Norton's Balanced Scorecard was the route to go. I spent the next few months training with them in Boston and New Orleans. I talked with consultants at the Balanced Scorecard Collaborative; read their book, *The Balanced Scorecard* (Harvard University Press, 1995); and networked with colleagues who had had success with it. We decided early on to pilot it in our Retail Banking Division, then roll it out to the rest of the bank. Well, this is pretty much what happened, though I will detail the keys to our success later. For the sake of introducing the challenge, let's make the following assumption:

Let's say we are all ready to roll it out, and I am the main trainer. I do, however, have other executives participating in the design and facilitation of a two-day session. We do a fine job of introducing and explaining it with success stories, illustrations, data, colorful PowerPoint slides, examples, audience participation, and even a skit or two. We make sure we link the building and use of our version of the balanced scorecard to our strategy, and to corporate, division, and department goals. Let's say the training went well and trainers received high reaction scores (Level 1), and all participants passed competency tests (Level 2). Now comes the first real test—*Will they apply it as we have directed and they have learned?* The challenge is strong, since they are no longer a captive classroom audience. The training team was, to this point, able to control the environment, who was invited, and our training methods. Now that the two-day training is over, they walk out the door and back to their jobs as division and department managers. We have lost our *control* and now must rely on *influence*.

What will happen with these balanced scorecard–enlightened managers? How many will implement it successfully? How long will it take? Personally, I don't like the odds of most of them taking what they have learned and effectively implementing this new management system— or any system, for that matter. Thus, the significant challenge is getting these managers to implement the balanced scorecard system in their areas and, in turn, get their associates to *learn* relevant balanced scorecard principles and *apply* those learnings to their everyday jobs.

THE GOOD NEWS

There is good news amid this challenge. The senior team at First Indiana Bank, including myself, was pretty certain that *if* we could figure out how to get this initiative successfully implemented, it would lead to significant corporate improvement. In other words, the challenge of moving from behavior (Level 3) to results (Level 4) was all but assured. So, the only real, significant challenge was moving from Level 2 to Level 3, since we already have Levels 1 and 2 covered.

Let me expand on that point. How many phone calls, e-mails, and brochures do you get each week promoting some sort of training? I get a lot. Many of them are interesting and potentially useful. Most of the time, I feel overwhelmed; I have too much to pick from. There are many more initiatives that we would like to implement than we possibly could. My point is this. There is a lot of great training material out there—information overload. Most of these models and methods for improved coaching, sales methods, customer service models, teambuilding, strategic planning, career development programs, and the like are effective to *the degree that they are properly implemented.*

THE CHALLENGE VIEWED FROM OTHER PERSPECTIVES

I believe that the more you understand the inner workings of this challenge, the better you will be prepared to attack it. To do that, I will draw verbal illustrations from three gigantic forces in society today—sports, weight loss, and training.

Just this morning, I was watching TV and saw several Detroit Piston basketball players being interviewed for their upcoming NBA championship series against the perennial winners, the Los Angeles Lakers. To a man, their responses to the proverbial question, "What do you have to do to win?" were almost identical. Richard Hamilton summed it up best: "Coach [Larry Brown] is always telling us that we have to play basketball the right way." Think about it. He didn't say anything about strategy, learning, motivation, or passion. He was echoing what every sports personality says, "We need to execute!"

Hamilton was then asked, "How many times does Coach Brown mention that to you?" He laughed and said, "Too many to count—probably thousands!"

(The philosophy must have worked. They disposed of the Lakers 4 games to 1.)

Similarly, I once asked one of the coaches of the Indianapolis (football) Colts, "How is your strategy this year?" He replied, "Oh, about as good as everyone else's." "Well then, how will you guys win the Super Bowl?" You guessed it—"The teams that *execute* their strategies will go the farthest." Put yourself in the coach's role. (You probably are one at work.) You basically have complete command over strategy, rules, and practices. Once the game starts, however, the final outcome is almost totally up to the players, your employees. The same is true of training—the transfer of learning to behavior.

Let's also look at the issue of weight loss and diets. I cannot fathom how many different diets, fat-burning pills, fitness machines, and how-to books are on the market guaranteed to help us lose weight. Imagine the amount of money poured into that industry each year. Many years ago, in another career, I led a weight loss group. The plan was three-fold and simple: (1) Eat reasonably (2) Get regular exercise at least three times a week and (3) Drink lots of water. I had about fifteen participants in the group and guess what the majority of each session was spent doing? Encouraging and supporting their positive behaviors. Challenging their excuses and increasing their adherence to the program. They all knew what they needed to do, and they knew it would work if they followed the program. They also knew it would take consistent discipline and effort.

Let's assume that somehow, everyone who was overweight found a way to understand (Level 2) and implement (Level 3) this three-pronged approach to losing weight. What would the results (Level 4) be? There would be lots of thin people and a huge financial loss to companies that sell diet books, special pills, and special weight loss foods. Why doesn't it happen?

WHAT WE'RE UP AGAINST—RESISTANCE TO CHANGE

We are up against human nature, which is an extremely powerful force. It is a commonly known fact that people tend to do what is familiar and comfortable, even if it is not effective. That's it in a nutshell. Hoping people—whether employees, athletes, or would-be weight losers—will voluntarily behave differently is not a reasonable expectation. If we are honest with ourselves and reasonably introspective, I'm sure we can look back at behaviors we continued or relationships we stayed in and wonder why we didn't change sooner. You may have heard the statement, "People don't mind changing. They just don't like to be told to change." I'm not sure how true that is, but it is another matter to consider when facilitating change.

A second human nature consideration is this: For trainers to get leaders to transfer learning to behavior, and for leaders to get their employees to transfer learning to behavior, *a lot of disciplined, consistent effort is needed.* Are you as aware as I am of how much society has moved away from that good old-fashioned work ethic? It's one of the reasons why most diets fail—people don't have the discipline or patience to consistently exercise and eat properly. I saw a commercial for fat burners the other day. I honestly don't know if they work or not, but I believe there are more and more products on the market that attempt to connect with our desire to make life easier. Whether or not they will depends on the successful transfer of Level 2 to Level 3.

It is my sense that here at First Indiana Bank, as well as in organizations and corporations elsewhere, the innovative thinkers often get more recognition and praise than do those leaders who maintain a steady course. I believe managers feel (and sometimes receive) pressure from senior executives to "do something" to increase customers, sales, and profits. That something often translates into a new program, project, product, or process. It takes discipline, courage, and hope to stay the course when those around you are not immediately satisfied with the results.

PART ONE—A FINAL WORD

You are up against a great adversary, human nature, if you truly want to overcome this challenge. It will take know-how, determination, and persistence on your part to defeat your worthy foe. This book details the know-how; the rest is up to you. I suggest you get a really good handle on how you want to attack this challenge, gather your able-bodied cobattlers, then deliberately move ahead!

PART II

FOUNDATIONS FOR SUCCESS

Abraham Lincoln was once asked, "If you had five hours to chop down a tree, how would you do it?" He allegedly responded, "I would spend the first four hours sharpening my axe." Thorough preparation and a firm foundation are essential to successfully meeting the challenge of transferring learning to behavior. It would be unfair and unreasonable to ask you to chop down a large tree with a dull axe. Similarly, it would be unfair of upper management, or of you yourself, to expect ultimate training success without certain prerequisites in place. I know of many situations in which expectations for consistent behavior change and subsequent positive results were doomed from the start. These next chapters serve to mention five of those foundations that, at least to some degree, need to be in place for you to be successful.
They are:

- A Strategic Focus
- The Right Kind of Leadership
- The Ability to Plan for and Manage Change Effectively

- An Effective Measurement System
- Success with Levels 1 and 2

As I mentioned earlier, when I first started with First Indiana, I was asked to implement a TQM culture. As I dig back into my memory and notes as to why that was relatively unsuccessful, I see problems with each of these foundations. To be honest, back in 1997, First Indiana Bank did not have a sound strategic focus. A strategic plan, yes; strategic focus, no. We were not aligned to plan for and manage change effectively, in part because we did not have a strong scientific approach or an effective measurement system. We had hard-working, dedicated leaders, but we were missing some elements of the right kind of leadership. These and other prerequisites for training and performance success will be outlined in the following three chapters, as will the steps we took to correct our errors. So get ready to learn how to sharpen your axe.

Chapter 3

Strategy and Leadership

A STRATEGIC FOCUS

SETTING THE STAGE

In 1997, First Indiana Bank was a fine bank for a lot of customers, particularly in Central Indiana. We were financially sound, perceived as caring and friendly to our customers, and a good place to work. We were not, however, strategically focused. First Indiana had been around in some form for over eighty years. We were steeped in tradition. "But that's how we have always done it" was frequently the response when change was suggested. We did go through a strategy planning process every year, but the end product was stamped "Confidential" and typically found itself in a Senior Vice President's desk drawer.

Our budget process was extensive, to say the least. After months of deliberation and modifications, the final outcome generally dictated where we would put our priorities and our resources. One of our problems was that we were trying to be all things to all customers and had little focus on exactly who and what we wanted to be. Many companies are driven by tradition and budget. The practice of trying to be all things to all people is very tempting and pervasive. In response to this, decision-makers are jumping at impressive vendor and consultant packages that promise higher sales, better customer or employee retention, executional excellence, or faster turn-around times.

A NOTE ABOUT VENDORS AND CONSULTANTS

Since I have broached the topic of vendors and consultants, I would like to offer some words of advice. I have worked for and with a number of professional consultants, and have been around enough to have seen the spectrum. Let's start with the downside. Watch out for over-promise, under-deliver. This is how that scenario typically unveils. A firm somehow gets your attention—either from a mailing, phone call, website, e-mail, or personal contact—inquiring about your training needs. You agree to meet with them ("but I only have an hour") and they show-and-tell you with an impressive presentation of what their products or services can do to enhance your training effectiveness. If you are impressed enough and find their offerings potentially beneficial, you set up another meeting with higher-ranking participants from both sides. So far, so good. To make a long story short, you agree to make the investment and begin the implementation process. There are several considerations you would have been wise to discuss before making that decision.

First, is the product or service based on an actual need that you have? Will it bring you tangible benefits that you couldn't obtain on your own or at a lower cost? Second, is what they are offering capable of aligning with your current technology, culture, and personnel? A company I worked with spent a ton of money on a state-of-the-art system that didn't fit with its technological infrastructure. It sure looked good when it was explained and demonstrated, but they finally had to abandon it and implement another, which put them three years behind schedule. My point is this: make sure the products and services you purchase are fiscally sound and aligned with your strategy. Also, be a careful shopper. Be sure that what you think you are getting is what you are actually getting. Finally, watch out for overly complex models, whether for strategic planning, new sales methods, service models, or whatever. Although the performance enhancement models being promoted today are impressive, many are too complex to be successfully implemented. If you have trouble understanding what you are looking at, a good rule of thumb is that it probably won't work. I have seen many new models and initiatives, and when they actually work well, four times out of five, the foundations and methods are quite simple.

I do see a positive trend in the field of outside consultants. More and more organizations and corporations are carefully checking out what they are getting for their money. Specifically, they want products and services that will enhance the implementation of their strategy, they want to and be able to drive and maintain the change without the constant help and expense from the consultants. Bottom line: if the initiative remains consultant driven, I don't like your chances of success. If it is ultimately internally driven, I do.

HOW IMPORTANT IS STRATEGIC FOCUS?

I am an avid freshwater fisherman. I often cross paths with other fishermen (both male and female) and usually engage in some light conversation. As everyone who fishes knows, the most frequently asked question is "Have you caught anything?" The most frequent answer to the most frequent question is "Well, I just started"—meaning they have been there for 45 minutes and haven't caught anything yet, but are ashamed to admit it. The second most frequently asked question is, "What are you fishing for?" The answer is usually "Whatever will bite." I can't stand that answer. Talk about lack of strategic focus! If you don't know specifically what species of fish you are trying to catch, how do you know where to go, what baits or lures to use, or what time of day or season is best? The answer is, you don't.

The same is true for business, whether it is for profit or not. I am on the board of directors for the American Red Cross of Central Indiana, and they absolutely know what kind of fish they are trying to catch. I mean, they know what they are dedicated to doing—saving lives! All of their programs, finances, meetings, and training align either directly or indirectly to that goal. My wife, Denise, is a registered nurse. She has been trained in CPR by the Red Cross. On December 27, 2002, I was playing indoor tennis with my dad Don, brother Ted, and son C. J. After a while of playing, Don sat down on a bench saying he wanted to rest and was feeling some "indigestion." Shortly after he sat down, he slumped over on the bench, with a lifeless look on his face. His heart had stopped and he wasn't breathing. I held him, hoping he would breathe, but he wouldn't. Quick action from C. J. brought Denise to the scene within a couple of minutes, and a 911 call from Ted summoned paramedics. Now was the time to see if what Denise learned (Level 2) from the Red Cross would transfer to behavior (Level 3) that would save Don's life (Level 4). For several minutes she worked on him, giving him enough oxygen to keep him alive and keeping his blood circulating until paramedics came and shocked his heart and got it started again. If she had not been able to apply what she learned during those 5 minutes, he would not be with us now.

So you see, the Red Cross' strong strategic focus prompted the state of Indiana to *require* yearly CPR training of all nurses, which allowed Denise to learn it, do it correctly, and save Don's life. We are all, of course, thankful for each day that he is with us—still fishing, golfing, and conducting workshops.

FIRST INDIANA BECOMES STRATEGY FOCUSED

In 1999, our top executives made a conscious and determined decision to become truly *strategy focused*. A good part of my job as the Organizational Effectiveness Manager was to find ways to make that happen. We decided to move ahead with the Balanced Scorecard approach, but learned from reading Kaplan and Norton's second book, *The Strategy-Focused Organization* (Harvard Business Press, 2000), that much more was involved than putting a bunch of scorecards together. Before that, we had to first take several steps toward becoming strategy focused. To develop the strategic and tactical measures needed for a scorecard, we first had to have a sound, focused strategy that *everyone* in the organization was familiar with and could relate to.

My first decision was *not* to make the same mistakes I made with the TQM initiative. Here's how we did it. First, I went to two Balanced Scorecard conferences put on by Kaplan and Norton's group, The Balanced Scorecard Collaborative. My boss, Marni, attended one as well. Her attending was a big deal! It signaled to everyone that she was going to learn about this whole process (Level 2), then get and stay actively involved (Level 3) in it.

Shortly after the second conference, I purchased ten copies of *The Strategy-Focused Organization*. I then led our senior team—CEO, President, and seven Senior Vice Presidents—in a study of the book. The study was much more than a book review. I gave them weekly reading assignments along with several discussion questions for them to prepare. The reason for doing this, of course, was to get them all interested, involved, and committed—something I failed to do with TQM. I asked challenging questions like these:

- What aspects of Chapter One do you take issue with?
- How well is your area currently applying "X" from Chapter One?

- What do you propose to do differently as a result of reading Chapter One?

The subsequent discussions provoked interesting and sometimes heated discussion, but that is what we hoped would happen. Out of the discussion came *commitments to change*.

Several core elements emerged from the book study that needed immediate attention. The first were the answers to two questions: What is our identity as a bank? How will we differentiate ourselves from our competitors? We did some really good axe sharpening with these. There were hours of discussion, disagreement, and finally consensus on the answers. We were to be *the* finest locally owned community bank in Central Indiana. We would differentiate ourselves by serving as *trusted advisors* to our customers. We developed a vision and mission statement that aligned with our differentiator, and then tackled the issue of what our primary strategy would be. From our conferences, book study, and good old-fashioned common sense, we decided on a strategy that we still affectionately call The Three Ds—Discovery, Delivery, and Dialogue. We defined *discovery* as determining our customer's initial needs; *delivery* as meeting those needs (and subsequent ones); and *dialogue* as the continued, consistent, ongoing discussions with customers to deepen our understanding of their needs and their understanding of our products and services. In this way, we are able to deliver (Level 3) on what we initially learn (Level 2) and commit to. We position ourselves to earn their trust, continue dialogue, and increase profits (Level 4).

TQM Flashback!

First Indiana did not establish a true strategic directive for implementing a TQM model. We had not identified how we differentiate our company from our competitors' (our differentiator) or our basic strategy. We knew TQM would help us be more efficient, but our quality initiatives were not truly customer driven. We did have a Total Quality Council, which made an earnest effort to aid in the corporate transformation to TQM, but the planning for and the leadership of the Council came from an outside consulting firm. This limited the amount of ownership our senior executives took for the initiative.

We identified several more significant steps before we could consider ourselves strategy focused. We knew we had some pretty strong silos within our organization. By silos, I mean that divisions and departments were basically operating vertically, in a command and control manner. Goals, initiatives, and incentive plans were set up by silo, and I'd be less than honest if I said there wasn't some turf defense. I hope at this point you are asking, "Gee, we experience a lot of that. How did you begin to break down the silos?"

SILO BUSTING

We decided to attempt to bust our silos not just for the heck of it, but because they were going to interfere with us accomplishing our vision, strategy, and goals. Here are the methods we used:

1. *We held a wedding.* What? Yes, we got a bit creative here. We rented a big church and sent out invitations to our 750 associates to a wedding at 5:30 p.m. on Thursday, April 15, 2001. We deliberately left off one detail on the invitations—who was getting married. At 5:20, individuals and small groups of associates began showing up at the church. They wondered who would be getting married in such an odd way, but no one figured it out. As they came inside, they were greeted by the Senior Vice Presidents (SVPs) dressed in tuxes and acting as ushers. Instead of the usual "Bride or Groom?" question, they asked each person "Sales or Service?" With the appropriate response, the ushers escorted the parties to one side of the church or the other. By 5:30, we had a full church, pretty evenly divided between sides. We then began the ceremony. I had been voted to be ring bearer, so the flower girl and I led the way, followed by our President representing Sales, and our Chairman Marni McKinney representing Service. Our Director of Retail Banking offered some choice words on what this marriage was all about. He explained that we no longer were going to be separate entities, but that today was the day that we would start this new life together. As I remember, he did a fine job of weaving in our mission, vision, differentiator, and basic strategy. Marni then led the two sides in an exchange of vows. I don't remember too much about that, but among other promises, the sales associates recited something about turning in complete applications, and the service associates vowed to reduce turn-around times among other things. Of course we had a reception immediately following to celebrate our new union. Ahead of all of us, however, lay the challenge of getting leaders and associates to transfer what they would learn into new behaviors.

At the time of this writing, we are still working on the marriage!

2. *We developed strategy maps.* These were visual representations of our strategy, constructed for the purpose of communicating strategy throughout the bank. The model we used came from Kaplan and Norton's *Strategy-Focused Organization*. It was not so much the four maps themselves, but the manner in which we built them—*by customer group instead of by division.* In other words, instead of a Retail Banking Strategy Map or a Commercial Banking Strategy Map, we chose instead to develop an Individual Customer Strategy Map and a Business Customer Strategy Map. This forced leaders and associates from different departments and divisions (different silos) to work together because they shared the same customer group. I must admit that this did not come easy. We had to do some quick targeted training to equip leaders and associates to be able to work in ways and with people that they hadn't in the past. We also found out that the strategy maps and subsequent balanced scorecards were great tools for prompting and tracking the transfer of learning to behavior using the four levels.

3. *Our meetings became more strategic and cross-functional.* Leaders from different departments frequently worked together on common opportunities or problems, especially after we were up to speed with all of our balanced scorecards. These meetings, consistent with a strategy-focused organization, focused largely on strategic execution. We adopted the general goal of *Executional Excellence*. Much discussion centered on the tactics and initiatives to accomplish that. Our leaders became skilled in leading multilevel and cross-functional teams, and even new strategies built in cross-functional components. I often referred to the four levels during these meetings.

4. *Our training also changed.* We began developing interventions that addressed customer impact issues as opposed to departmental training. We taught methods of working more effectively together, and spent a great deal of time and effort on better equipping our leaders. Again, the transfer of learning to behavior was a critical component built into each training program.

5. *We modified our incentive systems* to include some cross-functional and customer-oriented components, as opposed to the traditional approach of using individual metrics.

As I look back, I think we missed the boat on one opportunity— recognition. We continued to approach recognition and awards from an individual performance perspective. We are now modifying that approach to include more departmental and cross-functional teams.

CASCADING STRATEGY

When senior management sets the mission, vision, differentiator, and basic strategy, it is critical to communicate it throughout the organization and make strategy "everyone's everyday job," as Kaplan and Norton say. I hope you understand the importance of this. In order for strategy to be executed effectively, you need a critical mass of leaders and line employees to be committed to this comprehensive communication process. And they cannot be committed if they don't know what it is, and especially if they don't know how it relates to their jobs. At First Indiana, we don't do anything fancy with this. We do, however, make sure that every year our strategy is shown and explained to all levels of leaders, who in turn cascade it through the rest of the organization. Each manager spends time with his or her area and with individual employees to help them see how their individual efforts and contributions link to departmental and corporate strategy.

ENHANCING OUR STRATEGIC FOCUS

A model we also used early on in our quest to be more strategy focused came from a book by Brian Joiner called *Fourth Generation Management* (McGraw-Hill, 1994). Joiner's model, The Joiner Triangle (p. 11), illustrates the three components that must be balanced for strategy to be implemented effectively: Quality, Scientific Approach, and All One Team. Joiner defines *Quality* as "understanding that quality is defined by the customer" and involves taking deliberate steps to solicit, analyze, and utilize customer feedback and buying patterns; lip service will not do. *Scientific Approach* refers to "learning to manage the organization as a system, developing process thinking, basing decisions on data, and understanding variation." We carried the concept to hiring practices, models for process improvements, evaluating training effectiveness, and determining strategic objectives. Finally, *All One Team* means "believing in people; treating everyone in the organization with dignity and respect." I would often hear from managers that they were in great shape with All One Team: "Yes, everyone in my department works real well together." My response is, "Well, that's fine. But I consider that *all one team* [lower case]. All One Team really means working effectively cross-functionally, as well."

The reason I mention Joiner's Triangle is that it was a simple enough model for all of us to understand and make use of. It was very helpful to us in early stages of our journey to becoming strategy focused. Although the triangle did not directly help us develop and focus on strategy per se, it did help us balance things out so that we were better positioned to do so.

ALIGNING TRAINING WITH STRATEGY

A whole book could be written on the topic of aligning training with strategy (and many have). Once organizational strategy has been set and communicated, it is critical for your training departments, learning centers, or corporate universities to align themselves closely with this strategy. Over the past few years, I have attended and presented at several corporate university conferences and learned a lot. First Indiana recently went through a transformation from a training department (mine) and several independent departmental trainers to a corporate university. In a flash of creativity, I came up with the name, First Indiana University, following in the footsteps of hundreds of other organizations who have named their university after their organizations. We are aggressively tackling two basic aspects of the corporate university model as we move ahead:

- Developing comprehensive programs of learning, as opposed to a smattering of individual courses
- Utilizing a business consulting model

More will be said about First Indiana University later, as it helps us transfer learning to behavior and results.

WHAT CAN YOU DO TO IMPROVE STRATEGIC FOCUS?

Most, if not all, of the keys to success have to do with executive management. Sometimes, there is a true champion of learning and training on the senior team. Occasionally, one of you finds yourself in a position where you regularly meet with and influence that group. Often, however, neither scenario is the case. You may not have a lot of direct input or a true vote in major organizational decisions. You must, therefore, rely on *influence*. Here are a few suggestions for encouraging your senior team to make strategy a focus:

- Identify and suggest attendance at an appropriate workshop, and volunteer to set it up and go along.

- Recommend books to read, and perhaps volunteer to lead a senior team book review.

- Set up a luncheon meeting with members of your team and executives from other organizations that are further down the strategy road.

- Simply ask if they (individuals or the team) would allow you to share what you know about the importance of strategy focus.

- Draft and present a report that demonstrates the value of becoming more strategy focused, and the costs of not doing so. Do this in the form of a business case, including ways to measure results.

- And most importantly, keep asking questions that stimulate strategic thinking. Educate them about the four levels, and about the importance of the transfer from Level 2 to Level 3.

THE RIGHT KIND OF LEADERSHIP

Before jumping into this important prerequisite, I would first like to mention something about using the ongoing case study of First Indiana Bank. As you can probably tell, I am proud of who we are as a corporation and what we've accomplished. I believe the methods we have chosen to use are sound, but they are just one corporation's way of achieving success. I trust that the *principles* that form the foundation of those methods will work for you, but there is more than one road to Rome. As far as the individual methods, feel free to use those mentioned here. Perhaps even better, carefully review the case studies and best practices found in Chapters 9 and 10 of this book. All of these methods are tried and true. I am a practitioner first and foremost, and the methods explained in the case studies were submitted from professionals who *found them to work* as well.

Years ago, my boss gave me some advice that I have found useful to this day. "James, I am glad that you like to attend conferences. I trust you will learn a lot from the seminars and workshops. *But,* what I really want you to concentrate on is getting to know other professionals. Go out of your way to get acquainted with successful training leaders, and learn from them. After all, they have sifted through a lot of hype and theory and promise and have found what really works. Keep in contact with them, and make sure you find ways of reciprocating what you have learned."

AN EXAMPLE OF THE RIGHT KIND OF LEADERSHIP

I live in Indianapolis, the home of the Indianapolis Colts football team. During a recent televised football game, the Colts star running back, Edgerrin James, was interviewed. He was asked, "What is the difference between working with your old coach and your new coach?" James replied something like, "With our old coach, it was his way and he really didn't want to hear ideas from us [players]. With Coach [Tony] Dungy, if we have an idea as to how we might be a more effective team, he will listen to it. If he likes it, he will explore it and perhaps use it. If he doesn't, he will explain to us why it won't be used."

THE NEED FOR BALANCE

I met with two colleagues yesterday and discussed the need for the kind of balanced leadership that many of the world's best leaders practice. We specifically talked about the balance of support and accountability. I first asked them the question "What would it be like to work in an area where the leadership was primarily on the support side?" The response from one of them was "Oh, I suppose it would be pleasant enough, lots of recognition and encouragement. I'm not sure everyone would get along, however. There would be nothing to really hold the less internally motivated employees accountable. The more responsible ones, and the ones who respond well to support, would end up doing the work of those who didn't. I would also think that the productivity level for that department would be low."

I then asked them, "What would it be like to work in an area where the leadership was out of balance the other way, on the accountability side?" The other responded, "Oh, that would be just as bad or worse! I know of managers that behave that way. The atmosphere would be tense, and employees would feel constantly under the gun. There might be some periods of strong productivity, but it wouldn't last because people would get burned out and leave. Even the top performers would eventually crumble!"

Bingo on both counts. Can you see the result of strong imbalance? We must evaluate the need for this balance in terms of *impact* to our employees and, ultimately, to our customers. I believe we all have a tendency to lean one way or the other. Only occasionally do I find a truly balanced leader. I tend to be more into support. I have, however, worked hard the last few years on holding people more accountable.

There is one particular dynamic that I believe bears mentioning. We all know that the world economy has been tough, especially since the terrorist attacks in the United States on September 11, 2001. This has created pressure on individuals and organizations to perform. Margins are currently narrow; profits are slim; and not-for-profits are having trouble raising funds. This pressure is being felt throughout an organization, from the top down. As a result, many organizations and individual leaders are focusing more on the accountability side. This is understandable and may be necessary, but with it comes an alarming and often disguised downside. Every organization has its top performers, mid-level performers, and poor performers. Perfectionist managers, or those who feel strongly under the gun, tend to compartmentalize their employees into *two* groups instead of three. They see the top performers, and then everyone else; they start treating mid-level performers as poor performers. Expectancy theory tells us that we tend to behave as people expect. Mid-level performers begin to act tentatively, make more mistakes, and lose confidence because their manager is expecting them to fail. In other words, they start to *behave as if* they were poor performers instead of mid-level performers who just need support, encouragement, training, and coaching. It is a hard cycle to break, and becomes very expensive with the cost of constant employee turnaround. I suggest you watch out for this.

WATCH OUT FOR THE STOPPER

I have a good friend called Rich whom I tutored in the development and use of the balanced scorecard (BSC). At the time, he was working for a large real estate development company in the Midwest and thought that the BSC system would be extremely beneficial. He presented his plan to a small group of senior executives, who cut him short: "Sure. Go ahead and try it. Let us know if it works." Rich is a very proactive leader, so he quickly set out to implement it in his area. Rich is also very capable, and soon he had not only developed several balanced scorecards, but was able to get his entire staff committed to using it. So far, so good. An important component of the balanced scorecard management system is this: it works most effectively when it is linked to areas run by internal partners. Rich was in a service area, and asked for cooperation and involvement from sales, marketing, and other service areas. Well, the heads of those departments didn't appreciate Rich "meddling" in their areas, so they complained to the executive managers. Rich was stopped cold in his tracks. He was summoned to the boardroom and told not only to leave the other areas out of it, but also that it would probably be best "for all concerned" to go back to the old way of doing things. Rich was shocked. The president's parting words to him were, "Rich, we appreciate your efforts with the balanced scorecard, but had no idea that it would go this far."

Has anything like that ever happened to you? The *stopper* is senior management not being on board with your goals or plans. Before you conclude that I think this is the fault of executive management, I do not. It is *our* responsibility to check with executives often to ensure that we are "on the same page." If we continue without gaining their commitment, it is extremely demotivating as well as a big waste of time. I urge you to be cautious here. They may appear to be on board, but to be on the safe side, you should develop a thorough presentation to them, outlining your purpose, desired outcomes, cost-benefit analysis, resource requirements, and so forth. Not only can it save you and your team a big disappointment, but as you will see later, it will allow you to generate ownership and active involvement from those senior executives.

TQM Flashback!

We didn't do *everything* wrong with our TQM initiative. We did have the chairman of the bank, Marni, on the TQ Council, as well as a couple of other senior leaders.

AN EFFECTIVE LEADERSHIP MODEL

Just this past year, we found a leadership model that we really like. It is detailed in a book by Jim Kouzes and Barry Posner entitled *Leadership Challenge* (Jossey-Bass, 2002). I won't give you the details here, other than to list and briefly describe the five dimensions of leadership that they espouse:

- *Challenge the process.* Leaders *search for opportunities* to change the status quo and *experiment and take risks*.

- *Inspire a shared vision.* Leaders *envision the future* and *enlist others in their dreams*.

- *Enable others to act.* Leaders *foster collaboration* and *strengthen others*.

- *Model the way.* Leaders *set an example* for others to follow and set interim goals so that people can *achieve small wins*.

- *Encourage the heart.* Leaders *recognize contributions* that individuals make and *celebrate accomplishments*.

Now, back to the fishing analogy. Many fishermen are constantly on the search for the magic lure that will all but bring fish leaping into the boat. Some lures give off a special fish-attracting scent, others whistle, rattle, jiggle, send off vibrations, swim on their own, twirl around, swim backwards, resemble a tiny beer bottle, have whiskers and a tail, or light up in the dark. There are at least as many models of effective leadership. Kouzes and Posner's is the model we use at First Indiana. We believe it best fits the style of leader we want to develop and nurture. There are many other models, some equally as comprehensive and current, but my point is this. Although a sound model is important, just like sound strategy is, it is how it is *implemented* that makes all the difference. The right lure fished in the wrong way or wrong place will not work. Nor will the right leadership model that is left on the shelf or used in the wrong way.

LEADERSHIP DEVELOPMENT

Following is what we do to develop leaders and improve leadership behaviors. We believe that much of our First Indiana University resources should be directed toward our leaders. After all, *they are the key in attacking the challenge of transferring learning to behavior*! If I were speaking to a group, I would repeat that statement. Much of the training and coaching we offer our leaders is so they can support and use accountability to get our hundreds of associates to perform their jobs properly and effectively. But, we also want to ensure that these leaders and potential leaders are being developed for this training and coaching to stick.

I want to share with you not only the instrument we use to develop and challenge our leaders, but also the *process* we go through to do it. This is a process we learned this year from Dr. John Lovell, a consulting psychologist out of Fort Wayne, Indiana. Briefly, here is what we are in the midst of doing, step by step:

1. I purchased a sufficient number of copies of *Leadership Practices Inventory* 360° feedback instruments (at less than $60 a copy) for our leaders. This was developed by Kouzes and Posner.

2. We met with all of our managers (100) and explained the 360° feedback process that we would invite them to participate in. This was led by John Lovell, Marni, and me.

3. Our top executive, Marni, first completed the inventory along with her ten observers. Each observer filled out a questionnaire and answered three or four open-ended questions that Marni wanted specific feedback on. John and Marni facilitated a two-hour feedback process in which Marni received more feedback, examples, and support from all of her observers. All observers not only reviewed a copy of all of the results at the meeting, but also received a copy of her subsequent developmental action plan. By the way, all documents, except for Marni's and my copy, were shredded to protect confidentiality. She then developed an action plan and sent it to all her observers.

4. The rest of the senior team then went through the process. They each took part in a feedback session with our observers—boss, peers, and direct reports.

5. I then facilitated the third round for our directors and department managers.

6. With my guidance, everyone developed action plans that focused on ensuring that new behaviors (Level 3) would come from the insights gleaned from the feedback sessions (Level 2). Each participant's manager subsequently will offer periodic followup, feedback, and coaching.

It is working very well. The feedback instrument is important and helpful in sorting data, but the *actual feedback process* is when the real issues come out. Sessions are extremely candid, encourage the identified leader, and function as teambuilding events, as well.

EXECUTIVE INVOLVEMENT AND OWNERSHIP

Do you want your training to lead to new behaviors and positive results? If so, you will need to *solicit executive involvement*. Executives and department heads need to be involved for several reasons. First, involvement creates *ownership*. If they have a sense of ownership for a particular initiative or program, they will be much more likely to support it. An important principle to remember is that *involvement* generally leads to *commitment*, not merely compliance. Second, involvement creates *understanding*. Apply this to the four levels—without a good basis of understanding (Level 2), you can't expect them to show an interest and hold people accountable (Level 3). Third, executive involvement gives any training program more credibility, particularly if leaders are involved in the actual delivery of training.

Marni again served as a good illustration in an ongoing balanced scorecard class I was teaching. Wearing a Sherlock Holmes outfit complete with pipe, hat, and huge magnifying glass, and not saying a word, she slowly moved around the room, investigating various inanimate (and some animate) objects looking for clues of some sort. She then explained to the dumbfounded group that balanced scorecards can also yield clues to improve production and profitability.

TQM Flashback!

As I mentioned before, senior managers were included on the TQ Council. They seemed to understand what was going on with TQM, offered helpful suggestions, and made decisions to promote TQM in the future. But that was as far as it went. They did *not* attend the actual training. They did *not* conduct any of the training. They did *not* offer input into what reports would look at. They were *not* coached (by me) in how to support their people who had gone through the training. You can see what that all adds up to. Ugh—it hurts to think about it.

WHAT CAN YOU DO TO IMPROVE LEADERSHIP?

My professional contacts have offered the following suggestions that might improve your organization's leadership and get them actively involved in your corporate university or training department.

- Compel decision-makers to hire balanced leaders. Push for deliberate, scientific hiring processes.
- Thoroughly and tactfully prepare a presentation to senior executives outlining prerequisites, including their responsibilities, for overall training success.
- Put many of your resources into leadership courses such as development, selection and interviewing, feedback, managing change, and coaching.

- Conduct a business consulting needs assessment with key leaders.

- Develop and make effective presentations to key leaders. Include examples of all four levels to show the linkage to bottom-line results (i.e., demonstrate potential value).

- Continue to emphasize that they are the key element in ensuring that their associates successfully transfer what they learn in training and coaching to new behavior on the job.

- Persuade key leaders to attend learning activities and training before their people go through them.

- Bring key leaders in as "adjunct faculty." Get them to introduce or even conduct the training.

- Involve leaders in a mentoring program.

- Train and coach all leaders how to do effective followup with their trainees.

- Include the active support of training in leaders' job descriptions and incentive plans.

- Involve key leaders in the development of appropriate metrics for Levels 3 and 4.

Here is a technique I learned from a colleague I met at a conference in Toronto, Canada, several years ago. She called it an "On-Boarding Interview." I wish I could give her credit, but I can't locate her. It seems as though the company—let's call it ABC, Inc.—was having trouble with employee attrition. They are a world-renowned company with top-shelf training. As new employees neared the end of their training, recruiters from other companies would call them and entice them away. It was very upsetting, not to mention costly, since ABC gave their new employees such excellent training, only to have other companies take advantage of it. Here is what her company did to greatly reduce this turnover. Human Resources leaders were able to determine that employees most often left eight to ten months into their employment. So, after the employee had been with ABC for six months, an On-Boarding Interview was conducted. It was done in a one-on-one format by a senior executive of the company. This "involved and invested" executive set the stage for a candid, supportive discussion, and basically inquired about two things: How closely did their prehire expectations align with what they actually did experience during the first six months? What kind of support—clear expectations, feedback, coaching, work atmosphere, resources, etc.)—have they received during these first six months to help them do their jobs? These questions, to no surprise, often brought forth problems and concerns, as well as glowing reports. This was good news, however, as it served as an early warning system. Subsequent steps could then be taken to improve the satisfaction and loyalty of the employees *before* they became vulnerable to another company's solicitation.

FINAL THOUGHTS

I strongly suggest that you take an informal inventory of strategic focus and leadership support prior to undertaking any major training initiative. If there are significant gaps in either, be sure to talk with senior executives about them, and be sure to bring along proposed solutions. Make sure you link what your training is supposed to accomplish with specific behaviors you'd like to see from your executives. Finally, show them the critical cause and effect relationships of strategic training objectives, executive involvement, evaluation, and ultimate customer loyalty.

Chapter 4

Culture and Systems

AN EFFECTIVE CHANGE MANAGEMENT SYSTEM

I knew long ago that this topic would make the top five list of prerequisites to training. I just didn't know what change model I would espouse. After reviewing many models, I chose the one proposed in a book called *Managing Change Effectively* by Dr. Donald Kirkpatrick (Butterworth-Heinemann, 2001). I chose it for two reasons: (1) the model fit with my thinking and the rest of this book, and (2) I had a free autographed copy to refer to. I will get to the specific model later in this chapter.

IS YOURS A LEARNING ORGANIZATION?

I really like the term *learning organization*. To me, it says that the organizational culture is geared toward accepting innovative ideas, looking for strategic and tactical opportunities to make improvements, and has a critical mass of leaders and employees who are invested in learning. You can sense a spirit of learning whereby leaders know that planned, strategic change is a powerful way to increase productivity. Are you that kind of organization? If you are, you have the golf ball sitting up nicely on the tee, ready to help facilitate the transfer of learning to behavior. As a matter of fact, you can skip the rest of this section and just move on to the next. If, however, your organization can stand to improve in this area, read on.

TQM Flashback!

I believe there were several leaders and other participants on the TQ Council who were eager learners and embraced change as an ally, not an enemy. They (we) didn't, however, find the means to achieve critical mass with this issue. Many leaders in the bank were convinced that the courses they were on were the right ones and that there was no real need for change. One vivid example was the reluctance of several leaders to solicit scientifically gathered customer feedback. "Oh, we already know our customers like the back of our hand. Why do we need to spend money for some outside firm to tell us what we already know?"

LEARNING AND CHANGE

I teach a change management course both at First Indiana University and at the Indiana Institute of Technology's MBA program, where I am an adjunct professor. The ability to plan for and manage change effectively is closely linked to learning. The stronger the learning culture, the easier it is for a company or agency to move through the change process. As a training professional, you can engage in three specific steps to prepare the way for effective change.

1. *Assess to what degree yours is a learning organization.* Look for individuals, teams, or departments that are oriented toward learning and change. They are not hard to spot. Here are the kinds of things you will hear from them:

What can we learn from that experience?

See if you can find out why we lost that customer.

If we go that direction, what effect will it have on our internal partners?

What is your reaction to this?

Let's see if we can find a way to make that work.

Is there a pattern here?

Conversely, those who believe they have learned enough to get them through the rest of their working lives are the ones who tend to:

critique energetically a new idea (someone else's) in terms of why it won't work;

infrequently ask questions for clarification;

generally do more talking than listening;

have a hard time accepting responsibility when things don't go right; and

avoid conferences, networking, and reading new books.

2. *Design and deliver either a leadership-oriented or companywide course on planning for and managing change.* Include key "adjunct faculty" members in both facets. Use the individuals or teams identified in the first point above. Make sure you include ways to support and recognize those who choose to become more learning- and change-oriented.

3. *Build change and learning components into all the programs you conduct.* Make extra sure to include them in leadership development and coaching courses. Showcase successes whenever possible.

At First Indiana, I am in charge of setting the agenda for and facilitating something we call Indiana Group. This is a monthly gathering of all of our managers to discuss strategy and market trends, and to share best practices and recognize top performers. Our chairman and our president take an active role in the proceedings. They use this opportunity to present the rationale and plans for any major changes. They also consistently mention the need to apply (Level 3) what they learn (Level 2) in Indiana Group. The rest of us greatly appreciate hearing about the status of the organization and proposed changes straight from the top executives. One of the purposes of Indiana Group is to share best practices so that leaders in other departments are exposed to new ideas that they may choose to implement.

I don't know of any stronger reinforcer of new behavior than a testimonial from individuals or groups of employees about something that is working. I can think of a number of different manifestations of change that were showcased to the management team over the past

few years. One had to do with our conversion to the balanced scorecard system. We got off to a bit of a rough start with our new balanced
scorecards. Managers were selecting measures that they knew were at
or above targets. Sometime in 2000, I reviewed Barb Freeman's scorecard. Barb is a fine manager in our Secondary Marketing division. I noticed that one of her measures was well below target, and she had given
it a designation of "red," indicating that the processes associated with
it were "in need of help." I asked her if she was willing to share this in
the upcoming Indiana Group; she was. Well, I finally thought of a way
to dramatize the point, so as I was wrapping up another topic in the
next Indiana Group, I said, "Hey Barb. I'm sorry I didn't get a chance
to look at your scorecard like I promised. Is it OK if I take a few minutes and look at it right now?" She was in on the ploy, and said, "Sure."
I proceeded to put it up on an overhead for all to see. (There was an
uneasy rustling from the audience at this point.) Of course, I com-
mended her on a nice looking scorecard, and pointed out a few very
useful measures she had developed. Just as I was about to take it off the
screen, I pretended to notice the "below standard" measure. "Oh, Barb.
What is this? All the rest of these measures are either at or exceed target. What do you mean by including this one? Can't you do something
to make this look better?" You could have heard a pin drop. As I was
trying to figure out what to do next to drive my point home, our president at the time—jumped up and yelled, "Kirkpatrick! Leave her
alone! That is exactly what I want her to do! I am tired of everyone
cherry-picking measures so their areas look good." As I think back, I
sort of wish that I had let him in on the plan, because he was really
mad at me. But, he made his point, and I had made mine. A frank discussion followed, with a directive from the president that "from now
on I want useful measures and honest metrics on all scorecards." He
also promised not to overreact to measures that didn't meet standards.
Two things changed after that: He kept his word and worked proactively with managers to facilitate improvement in below-standard
measures, and managers changed their measures to those that had true
strategic and tactical importance, regardless of how "good" they
looked.

   Over the months and years of Indiana Group and of various strategy
and operating committee meetings, best practices have been shared by
countless individuals, departments, and cross-functional teams. Believe me, the impact of peers and coworkers getting up and proclaim-
ing the benefits and results of implemented change is far more powerful
than anything I could say. My role was to find these people and help

them prepare for their big moment. There is a side benefit to doing this, as well. It offers senior and junior leaders in the bank a chance to see the fine work of these individuals and teams and to learn that the axiom that *visibility leads to advancement* has come true on many occasions.

TQM Flashback!

We didn't think to invite individuals and teams to highlight TQ successes in front of this and other groups. I wish we had!

A LEADER'S MODEL FOR CHANGE

Most of the following comments and model is taken from Don's book, *Managing Change Effectively*.

To manage change effectively, a systematic approach is required. The following seven steps should be followed to ensure that the best decisions are made and that the changes will be accepted by those involved.

Step 1: Determine the Need or Desire for a Change

This can be done in many ways. For example, based on facts or feelings, top management can determine that change is needed. Or a manager, whether based on personal observation or on suggestions from direct reports and/or others, can decide there is a need for change. Typically, data exist to back up the need or opportunity for change.

Step 2: Prepare a Tentative Implementation Plan

Brainstorming, prioritizing ideas, and developing a tentative plan occurs at this step. Emphasis should be on the word *tentative*—subject to change. It is important at this step that those who develop the tentative plan are open to change and do not take a defensive attitude when reactions are negative or modifications are suggested. To be open-minded at this point is a prerequisite for the effective imple-metation of the change. Otherwise, those who have other ideas will recognize that their input is not really being considered. The consequences will be a reluctance to speak freely and resentment for being asked, yet not listened to. This may ultimately lead to *compliance* but not *commitment*.

The plan should always include steps to ensure that new behaviors result from learning.

Step 3: Analyze Probable Reactions

Almost every proposed change will be met with one of three different reactions. Some people will resent and possibly resist the change if it is implemented. Some people will remain neutral; they couldn't care less whether the change is made, or they will adopt a wait-and-see attitude. And others will accept and possibly welcome the change. At this point, it is important for managers to understand the individuals who will be involved. An empathic and supportive approach to others working through and getting used to the idea of change is critical.

Step 4: Make a Final Decision

The final decision should be made after comparing plans and approaches that have been considered. The brainstorming mentioned in Step 2 can produce many other options to consider. The reaction to a tentative plan can also help in making a final decision. At this point, leaders must decide whether they will make the final decision and move on with implementation, or use a group problem-solving approach. Neither is best all the time, and the decision must be deliberately thought out.

Step 5: Establish a Timetable

Sometimes the change is a simple one and can be implemented in one step. Other changes may be complicated and require some sort of change process or project plan. For more complex changes, a timetable with resources, action steps, and deliverables is probably the way to go.

Step 6: Communicate the Change

Although it is listed as Step 6, communication is a continuous process that begins in Step 1. It must be a two-way process—telling and selling the plan, as well as listening to reactions and suggestions. When the final decision has been made and a timetable has been established, a thorough, planned communication approach is necessary.

Step 7: Implement the Change

This is the action step in which the final decision is implemented according to the timetable established in Step 5. Continuous evaluation is an integral part of this step. If the change is not proceeding as planned and resistance is evident, it is important to pause and objectively evaluate the situation before proceeding. A measurement system utilizing the four levels is very helpful at this stage.

WHAT CAN YOU DO TO MANAGE CHANGE MORE EFFECTIVELY?

I trust that many training leaders and executives will follow these seven steps or use a similar methodology—many, but not all. I continue to teach my change management courses because many managers think they can just plow ahead with changes and get maximum acceptance and results. I often hear, "This is a great course, but I wish *my* manager was here to hear this." Some managers think that there is no time to go through all these steps. True, we are all extremely pressed for time, but following these steps often makes the difference between success and failure of a new initiative. Unfortunately, managers who do not believe in involving participant input don't see the reason for the failure. Instead of seeing their failure to get acceptance and commitment, they typically blame it on "incompetent employees" or "noncooperative internal partners."

Training leaders can do much to indoctrinate these principles. First of all, you can work with managers who are less than enlightened about the great challenge of change. Bring in plenty of data, examples, and tact when you attempt to convince them of the dynamics that create either resentment and partial compliance (at best) or commitment. Second, teach a course in change management, as I do, making it as relevant as possible. If you reach enough people, critical mass will soon put pressure on those who have yet to adopt an effective change management approach.

Don's book does a great job of identifying and describing what he calls "the three keys to successful change—Empathy, Communication, and Participation." No course is complete without these elements. Be sure to include leaders as "adjunct faculty." Third, work hard with "enlightened" senior executives not only to participate in training, but also to conduct one-on-one coaching sessions with their direct reports. I have done this on occasion, and I know that any data, evidence, selling points, and so forth that I can provide are always appreciated. Gathering and showing data to executives that *demonstrates impact* is especially powerful and useful. Marni typically asks me to make a cost-benefit analysis of any major change I propose. She especially likes to see what the cost is not only if we *do* go through with it, but also if we *don't*.

Many of you are in the business of changing organizational or corporate cultures. I empathize with you, since that is the business I am in. I know how difficult it is. Your work at creating a culture that manages change well will pay strong dividends when it comes to transferring learning to behavior.

TQM Flashback!

I am afraid that these methods were not followed very well with the TQM fiasco. I still believe that the TQM model we chose was a good one, but there was not much in the way of inviting and integrating input and suggestions from stakeholders. We did include input from senior managers, but basically ignored the concerns and suggestions by middle mangers—those who would be responsible for actually implementing and supporting TQM. The subsequent results of less-than-hoped-for success were not surprising.

AN EFFECTIVE MEASUREMENT SYSTEM

I have always wanted to live on a lake, but so far haven't been able to pull it off. I do, however, have a small farm pond behind our house. It is not a thing of beauty, but it just so happens that the pond has a bunch of fish in it—big fish. I also have some children and grandchildren who like to come over and fish with me in "Grandpa's Pond."

I also have a small, two-story red barn just behind our house. The grandchildren have named it "Grandpa's Barn." (By the way, they call our house, "Nana's House." Hmmm, something to contemplate.) Anyway, there is a map hanging on the wall in Grandpa's Barn of Grandpa's Pond. I wish I could include a copy of this map in this book, but I'm afraid it is much too detailed to be given justice in a standard-sized book. I believe it would pass any Six Sigma, ISO 2005, or Malcolm Baldridge standard of measurement. My wife considers it ridiculous.

Let me describe it. There is, of course, the actual map of the four-acre pond, drawn to detail and scale. There are small, colored, and numbered shapes in various spots around the lake—some are scattered, some are clustered in particular places. These shapes—triangles, squares, and circles—have letters in them: C for catfish, B for bass, and *b* for bluegill. These symbols represent fish that were caught and released by members of the Kirkpatrick fishing contingent. Directly beneath the map is a grid that includes date, time, species, weight, length, bait or lure, and who caught the fish. It is all neatly organized into a format that Denise refers to as "running it into the ground." There is a different map for each year.

This map serves several purposes. First, it is a great visual representation that depicts our fishing strategy, and it gives any who view it a quick, easy-to-understand way to see and interpret results. Second, it serves as a motivator. Everyone wants to get their name on Grandpa's Map of Grandpa's Pond in Grandpa's Barn. And they all—my daughter Christa, in particular—want to see the biggest fish listed alongside their name. Third, it allows us to plan for the future. We can study last year's map and have a pretty good idea what methods and area of the pond might work for a given time this year. These uses demonstrate what I consider the most important purpose of measurement—*to make strategic and tactical decisions in the present and future.* As a side note, one of the reviewers of the manuscript of this book suggested that perhaps all this map stuff might take away the joy of fishing. I considered that and decided to pitch the map for this year and just have fun.

If you do as good a job of measuring your processes, projects, exceptions, turn-around time, customer feedback, and outcomes as I do measuring fish, you will be in fine shape. I do understand that most of you probably have an excellent measurement system in place. I also believe, however, that even if you do, you might not be maximizing the use-fulness of your numbers. In other words, your numbers might be sophisticated and accurately reflect organizational reality, but you may not be translating that information into solid analysis and prudent decisions. I also know of many companies that measure a lot of activity, but fail to measure effectively and comprehensively, missing the benefit of a system like the four levels. They especially ignore measures of behavior (Level 3). Therefore, I include this element in my short list of prerequisites to training effectiveness and performance improvement.

I think we do a pretty good job of measuring what is important at First Indiana. Our new president wants us to know our numbers. By this, he means he wants us to accurately monitor and record important information about our processes and results, as well as the activities of our competition. Only when we have accurate and comprehensive information can we make the right decisions for the future.

THE BALANCED SCORECARD

We use a number of methods and software systems to measure, organize, and report data, but our primary tool is the balanced scorecard (BSC). Every month, leaders from different divisions, departments, and banking centers (branches) generate as many as seventy-five balanced scorecards. Ours are designed to isolate key elements that leverage our corporate strategy. As you will see in an upcoming BSC sample, these measures all fit on one page, following the philosophy of *Do a few things and do them well.* The idea of BSCs is to translate strategy into action. As mentioned earlier, there are many effective ways of measuring and managing a business or agency. This one works well for us, so I will detail it in the next few pages, with special emphasis on *linking training to strategy.* In our case, we also use ours to display and monitor measures that represent all four training evaluation levels.

BALANCED SCORECARD FOUNDATIONS

We believe that to monitor accurately how effectively strategy is being implemented, we need to look at more than just monthly or quarterly financials. We build measures into our scorecard that show not only how well we have done (outcome measures), but also how well we are doing the things that will get us where we want to be (drivers). These can also be described as lag (outcome) and lead (drivers) measures. Each line consists of the specific strategy, the BSC category, a description of the measure, the actual measure, and the desired target. We use time frames of monthly, quarterly, and year-to-date.

The balanced scorecard we use, adapted from Kaplan and Norton, has four categories—*Financial/Production, Customer, Internal Systems,* and *Learning and Growth.* These are what is "balanced" in the balanced scorecard. Below is a description of each of the categories:

Financial/Production—These measures are bottom-line numbers, either financial or production, that are desired or required by shareholders. They can include measures of volume, income, budget, and production efficiency.

Customer—These measures correspond with customer buying or involvement patterns (what customers *do*) and customer survey information (what customers *say*). This category can include measures of customer loyalty, training reaction scores, customer referrals, and number of new accounts opened.

Internal Systems—This is where we need to excel to deliver quality products and services to our customers. In my modification of Kaplan and Norton's model, Internal Systems includes two predominant types of measures: *behaviors* such as the number of appointments set with prospects, profiling new customers, joint sales calls, and conducting coaching sessions; and *quality* measures such as turn-around times, customer impact errors, and percent of the time fees are waived.

Learning and Growth—These measures track the foundational initiatives that must be in place for us to be successful in the present and future. We organize them into four possible groups: *strategic information* such as new market data; *strategic competencies* such as new leadership skills; *strategic technology* such as a new loan origination system; and *climate for action* such as employee satisfaction or turnover measures.

Obviously, we must start from the top, financial/production, because we get those goals and targets from senior management. However, the logic of these four categories is clearest when you start from the bottom and work up. Here is how the logic flows: *Learning and Growth* objectives and measures tell us what we need to have in place to perform in an effective manner, described in *Internal Systems*, so we can please our *Customers*, which in turn leads to successful *Financial/Production* outcomes. In other words, we start from the top when *determining* strategy and how we will implement it, but we start from the bottom when we *develop* the plans to execute strategy.

Are you sort of following me? If not, try reading that last section again. If yes, keep going. The BSC sample will complete your understanding (Table 2).

BUILDING BALANCED SCORECARDS

We actually build these scorecards using the following major steps:

1. Develop *strategy maps* that depict overall organizational *strategic themes*.

2. Develop corresponding *strategic objectives* from the strategic themes, probably several objectives per theme.

3. Develop corresponding *measures* for each of the strategic objectives.

Table 1.

Strategic Theme	Strategic Objective	BSC Measure
Increase employee retention	Increase employee recognition	Number of kudos entered into system
	Increase employee satisfaction	Employee survey score
	Increase manager/ employee engagement	Percentage of managers completing course Number of engagement coaching sessions

For a specific example of how we go about building our balanced score-cards, let's start with an area familiar to all of you, a training program to increase employee retention. Table 1 illustrates the point.

Note how one strategic theme—increasing employee retention—generates three different objectives that, if executed properly, will lead to improvement. The corresponding four measures let us know how well this strategy is going, culminating in the obvious production measure of employee retention.

A MANAGEMENT SYSTEM

Keep in mind this system is a *system of management*, not merely a measurement system. If you are in the midst of making a change to a system similar to this and you hear managers say, "Oh, this is just a new way of reporting old numbers," know that they don't get it. You might not be explaining it clearly enough. My father often talks and writes about training being both a *science*—concepts, theory, principles, and techniques—and an *art*. That same principle applies to any system of management or measurement, including this one. The science is building the actual strategy maps and scorecards; the art is modifying, improving, and getting people to use them effectively.

WHAT IS "BALANCED" ABOUT A BALANCED SCORECARD?

I mentioned before that the four categories—financial/production, customer, internal systems, learning and growth—themselves work to make this system balanced. Other factors contribute to the balance as well: long- and short-term measures, owned and shared measures (e.g., shared with other lines of business), and balance within a particular category (e.g., a balance of behavioral and quality measures within *Internal Systems*, a balance of customer behaviors and survey responses within *Customer*).

LINKING THE BSC TO KIRKPATRICK'S FOUR LEVELS

Each division and department in First Indiana Bank obviously measures much more than can fit on a one-page scorecard. But the scorecard serves as a nice snapshot of the measures that truly drive strategy. For any service area, including training, it is mostly about *leveraging intangibles into tangibles*. I am defining "intangibles" as factors that cannot easily be directly and invariably linked to results. This is very similar to Kirkpatrick's four levels. The relative intangibles of training and learning are found in Kirkpatrick's Levels 1 and 2. Those same intangibles are found under learning and growth. To be successful, we must leverage the somewhat intangibles of Levels 1 and 2 into tangible behaviors and results (Levels 3 and 4).

ILLUSTRATING THE FOUR LEVELS IN A BSC

Let's continue with the example of increasing employee retention. To do so, the following example shows what must take place in each BSC category. Note also the corresponding levels of evaluation.

Two principles are crucial to understanding this chart and the BSC system as a whole. First, the measures listed here have been determined to be the key ones that will leverage success with the business objective of improved retention. This is all about *focusing the efforts* of an organization on what really matters—executing strategy. Second, these measures illustrate the *cause-and-effect relationships* between the measures. Chapters 7 and 8 will discuss how to demonstrate the value of training to executives (which, by the way, is another of training's great challenges). Cause-and-effect relationships—showing how the intangibles of training lead to tangible bottom-line results—are critically important to this understanding.

Table 2 illustrates both of these points. To explain the cause-and-effect relationships, one must start at the bottom and work up. Here is how it works with this example: Effective training is essential for learning to occur. Effective training can, in part, be measured by reaction

Table 2.

Line	BSC Category	BSC Measure	Rationale	Evaluation Level
1	Financial/Production	Employee retention	This is what we ultimately want to improve.	Four
2	Customer	On-boarding interviews conducted	These interviews are conducted by senior managers and will help identify problems early so that corrective action can be taken in time to reduce turnover.	Three
3	Customer	Level 3 evaluation scores	This is a measure of targeted manager scores that indicate that they are engaging their employees.	Three
4	Internal Systems	Manager coaching sessions conducted by trainers	This is the kind of followup behavior trainers must do to encourage change.	Three
5	Learning and Growth	Managers certified as coaches	Managers have had to learn and behave differently to be effective retention-focused managers.	Two (learning) Three (behavior)
6	Learning and Growth	Reaction scores for training conducted to teach managers how to engage employees	Effective training is a prerequisite to positive, employee-retaining behaviors by managers.	One

scores (Line 6). Line 5, the percentage of managers who are currently certified as "retention-focused managers," is a combination of learning (Level 2) and on-the-job application (Level 3). A high percentage indicates the degree to which this behavior has occurred. Line 4 illustrates the critical followup behavior that trainers must do to convert managers' new retention-focused behaviors into business as usual—regularly coach their employees through observation and feedback. This measure belongs in the *Internal Systems* BSC category because it is made up of behaviors that must come from the training department.

As we move up, Line 3 gives us a picture of ongoing new Level 3 behaviors that result from the training and coaching. This measure falls under the BSC category of *Customer* because it comes from what the training departments' *internal customers* (managers) do. Line 2 depicts another key behavior (Level 3) that must come from another internal customer, executive managers.

Here is how I would describe this picture to a (hopefully) wide-eyed executive whom I am trying to persuade to adopt this method: Note the *cause-and-effect* references throughout. "Kelly, you have said that one of your primary business challenges for 2005 is improving employee retention. Here is how my department will drive that. Starting at the bottom [point to Line 6], you note that we will first offer a series of exceptional training classes and plan to get high reaction scores. When that is successful, we will push for managers to demonstrate their learning and ability to be retention-focused leaders, as indicated by the percentage of them becoming certified here [point to Line 5]. When we have enough critical mass there, my department will continually offer coaching and followup [point to Line 4] to help those new behaviors stick. The cause-and-effect relationship then continues to Line 3 [point], which will tell us to what degree these trained, certified managers are actually *practicing* the new behaviors. If we can then get you and the other executives to conduct regular onboarding interviews [point to Line 2], retention will increase [point to Line 1]. Isn't it wonderful?!?!?"

Not only does this type of system and explanation demonstrate how and when training is effective in generating results, it also serves as an excellent method to *ensure* effectiveness. You see, the measures in Lines 6 through 2 serve as *early warning indicators*, not unlike the trouble lights in an automobile, so that mid-course corrections and interventions can be made to stay on target.

A SAMPLE BALANCED SCORECARD

Now it is time to put it all together for you. Figure 1 is an example of what a Training and Development Department or a Corporate University may develop for their balanced scorecard. If you study it, you will see examples of these cause-and-effect relationships.

I would like to point out a couple of nuances I have added to the basic Kaplan and Norton model.

Figure 1.

Fourth National Bank

2004 Balanced Scorecard—Training & Development

"Raise questions. Seek information. Make strategic decisions."

Month: July 2004

Manager: Kirk Patrick

No.	Strat.	Category	Monthly Results			
A		**Financial/Production Measures:**	**Actual**	**Target**	**Status**	**Chng.**
1		Profitability (EPS)	1.62	1.72	C	–
2		Customer retention	88%	94%	C	–
3		Customer loyalty (willing to refer)	72%	85%	NH	nc
4		Employee retention	92%	92%	OT	+
5		Employee loyalty (planning to stay)	95%	95%	OT	+
6		Training cost per employee	$230	$200	C	–
7		Department expenses	$320k	$300k	OT	nc
B		**Customer Measures:**	**Actual**	**Target**	**Status**	**Chng.**
1		Cross-sell ratio	6:1	4:1	C	–
2		Profile quality	65%	90%	NH	new
3		Manager followup to training	90%	95%	C	–
4		On-boarding interviews conducted	40	42	OT	+
5		Level 3 evaluation scores		TBD		
6		Business consulting requests	14	12	OT	nc
C		**Internal Systems Measures:**	**Actual**	**Target**	**Status**	**Chng.**
1		Observations of coaching sessions	16	14	OT	+
2		Manager coaching sessions conducted	16	15	OT	nc
3		Internal needs assessments conducted	9	6	ET	+
4		KUDOS written	12	18	NH	–
5		90-day delinquent (new courses)	20%	10%	NH	–
6		Courses cancelled	5	6	OT	nc

No.	Strat.	Category	Monthly Results			
D		**Learning & Growth Measures:**	**Actual**	**Target**	**Status**	**Chng.**
1		Managers certified as coaches	40%	50%	C	+
2		Employee certified—profiling	40%	40%	OT	nc
3		Trainees passed competency tests	95%	95%	OT	nc
4		Trainee reaction scores	4.80	4.50	OT	+
		New course development				
5		a. Upward coaching	98%	100%	OT	
6		b. New supervisors	80%	80%	OT	
7		Training tracking project	70%	80%	C	

Exceeds Target	=ET	Better	+
On Target	=OT	No Change	nc
Caution	=C	Worse	−
Needs Help	=NH	New Measure this Qtr.	new

1. I have added a category called "Strat," short for "strategy." We use this category to add numbers representing specific corporate strategies to show that each measure is linked to strategy. For instance, the number A1 for a given measure might correspond to the strategic objective of "increased employee retention."

2. Note the designations under "Status." At First Indiana, we actually use colors to represent each of the following status determinations:

Lavender = Significantly Exceeds Target

Green = Meets Target

Yellow = Caution (somewhat below target)

Red = Needs Help

This is a common way BSC users show how well they believe the measure is currently performing. This method forces managers to review the numbers on their scorecards and assess progress based on both objective data and information and such subjective considerations as market conditions, staffing, and competing priorities. The color system appears to be a much more effective approach than just variance calculations, because managers must defend the colors they choose. It also presents a vivid representation of how well strategy is being executed.

3. I also added a column called "Change." This simply shows if the measure has improved, stayed the same, or gotten worse since the last report.

Chapter 7 will contain a line-of-business scorecard with other modifications, tips on persuading line-of-business managers to include training-related measures on their scorecards, and how to get the most benefit from this type of system.

TQM Flashback!

We generally did a good job of measuring, especially the details of specific associates' processes. They measured and reported results against standards. We did not, however, measure the behaviors (Level 3) that would have supported this initiative. These behaviors should have included both supervisory support and compliance with developing flow charts and standards. We also did not effectively measure Level 4 results.

WHAT CAN YOU DO TO IMPROVE THE WAY YOUR ORGANIZATION MEASURES AND EVALUATES?

It does little good to talk about these prerequisites to training and performance success unless we can do something about them. The same is true for this one. Following are suggestions that can help you strengthen this prerequisite within your organization:

Meet with senior executives and department heads to emphasize and illustrate:

The importance and methods of evaluating training

The importance and methods of linking training to strategy

The concepts and examples of leveraging intangibles into tangibles

How aligning measurement methods with strategy will improve focus.

Draft a balanced scorecard or similar management and measurement tool for your area. Use it and show senior managers the benefits of it. Utilize the four levels within it.

Take an existing balanced scorecard from an area outside of your own and "mock it up" with some training measures. As you show the area manager, be sure to tell him or her how your area will help with those measures. Make sure you select a manager whom you think will understand and is likely to adopt it. As they find success, invite them to show other peers.

Invite someone from the outside to conduct a show-and-tell workshop on the balanced scorecard or a similar useful tool.

Good measuring isn't of much use unless it leads to meaningful reporting and subsequent decision-making. Work to develop and educate in these areas, and set an example that others can emulate. Emphasize the four levels and the transfer of learning to behavior.

FINAL THOUGHTS

Seek out true learners in your organization. They are the ones with the can-do attitude. Include them as you design programs, deliver training, and meet with the internal leaders you are trying to persuade to new ways of thinking and behaving. Transform these learners into leaders, as they will positively influence others with whom they come in contact. As with strategy and leadership, it is important to communicate to executives the necessary linkage of learning, the ability to proactively change, and measurement and reporting to the successful execution of corporate strategy.

Chapter 5

Success at Levels 1 and 2

During the first year of our marriage, I was extremely excited to share with Denise some of the joys of life that I had experienced. Two that specifically come to mind are fishing and golf. As a good and sensitive husband and a keen judge of character, I could tell that she was ecstatic to learn both without her even having to tell me. Although I did have an arsenal of other equally scintillating sports and activities at my disposal—camping, canoeing, basketball, and butterfly catching—I limited our first year to those two. After all, how much fun can a new bride stand?

We started with fishing. I thought it would be good to start early, so we started on our honeymoon. After all, my parents went fishing in Canada on their honeymoon. Well, I bought her fine fishing equipment and patiently showed her how to bait her hook, cast, and reel in the fish. I taught her what the different species looked like. I cleaned and cooked a few for her to eat. I even showed her how not to be afraid of an alligator or spiders when they attack your boat (unfortunate honeymoon incidents). Besides Florida, I took her to some other really nice places, including the Canadian north woods. But the subsequent results were puzzling to me. After a couple of years she stopped going fishing. She gave her fishing pole away. She didn't even want to come along with me when I went.

Well, being a husband who was fully devoted to his wife's pleasure, I suggested that we try golf. After all, what could possibly be not to like about golf? Again, I was the consummate teacher. I bought her some golf clubs at a flea market, cleaned the dirt off them, and took her to a nice big field where the first lesson began. I showed her how to position her feet, how to grip the club, and taught her about eagles, birdies, and pars. We went to a golf driving range where she got to hit a bucket of balls, with me as her constant, caring tutor. I showed her the "right way" to do it and was sure that the only reason she wasn't smiling was because she was concentrating so hard. The day finally came when we went to the golf course for the first time. As the morning progressed, I faithfully stayed at her side, helping her with every shot. I applauded what she did well, and counseled her when she didn't. I thought that everything was going smoothly and that we had found a sport that we could truly share together. I was wrong. On the next to last hole, I helped her line up her feet a bit so her putt would go straight. To my great surprise, she backed away from the ball, looked me straight in the eye, and said, "Jim. I know you are a gifted teacher. But if you give me *one more word of advice*, I am going to quit and never play again!" I am only human, and on the next (last, literally) hole, I very gently and caringly suggested that she "not walk in front of the man who is about to hit." I also remember tenderly tugging on her shirt a little to steer her away from him. Boom! That was it. She very calmly but deliberately picked up her golf bag, walked toward the car, deposited her nice set of clubs, bag and all, in the club dumpster, got in the car, and sat. *What went wrong?*

If I had known about the four levels at the time, I believe I could have figured it out. I was unsuccessful at Levels 1 and 2. I wonder if she would have appreciated a short talk on the four levels on the way home, or what kind of marks she would have given me on a Level 1 reaction sheet, or if she would have passed a Level 2 golf competency test? One thing is for sure: Levels 3 and 4 were a disaster. She never *played* (Level 3) in line with what I was trying to "teach" her, and if the desired *results* (Level 4) were for us to fish and golf together into our sunset years, it isn't happening.

As a postscript, I really did learn some valuable lessons during those early years. Suffice it to say that I reserve my teaching mode for the classroom, and try to find activities we would mutually enjoy through discussion, not by working my own plan.

SUCCESS AT LEVEL 3 DEPENDS ON SUCCESS AT LEVELS 1 AND 2

It is unrealistic to expect a change in behavior if appropriate learning hasn't occurred. And it is unrealistic to expect learning to occur if steps haven't been taken to create a positive learning atmosphere. That is why I caution training leaders not to address more sophisticated results, including Return on Investment, if they have not attended to the lower levels.

Denise did not want to learn to fish or golf. Neither sport interested her, but she was too kind to say so. I was working from *my* agenda, with *my* methods, and the vision of us fishing and golfing well into the twenty-first century was *my* vision. She was not motivated to learn, was not comfortable with my approach, and had little or no input in how and where we would do these things. Since she was not a *motivated or satisfied participant*, she most certainly was not truly receptive to learning either.

Let's look at the first two levels, and see what training prerequisites will help ensure a successful transfer of learning to behavior.

LEVEL 1: REACTION

At First Indiana Bank we modeled our Corporate University after a number of other organizations. One company in particular, Envision Financial, a fine credit union in Langley (near Vancouver), British Columbia, Canada, provided me with timely advice and friendship. I am indebted to Carol Hama, Jeanette Genge, and their entire team. As I mentioned previously, there are two basic components to First Indiana University: curricula offering comprehensive training and learning opportunities, and a business consulting approach. Both are based on needs that have been expressed (sometimes boldly; sometimes after some probing) by lines of business or other support areas of the bank. *This is the start of Level 1:* Training programs must align with business needs for managers to find them valuable. Those managers are more likely to support attendance by their employees. We conduct internal needs assessment with internal customers, then develop courses and interventions accordingly. We are careful to identify who these internal customers are, typically trainees, their managers, and senior executives.

START WITH ATTENDANCE

Current human resource development (HRD) research tells us that attendance is one component in the formula to measure business results. Getting the right people to the right training at the right time is a great challenge. We accomplish this by making the training interesting and relevant, by involving area managers in the development and delivery of it, and by soliciting executive leverage. Then we measure it on our monthly balanced scorecard.

EVALUATING REACTION

The business consulting model briefly described above brings Level 1 considerations into play during course development. Much can be done to enhance and evaluate reaction *during* training as well as afterwards. I have two good training friends that I want to tell you about. Dale Sears is a management consultant who works out of Indianapolis. He frequently finds time to stand in for me for one of my Indiana Institute of Technology MBA classes when I am out of town. Dale, a gifted consultant and motivational speaker, is a master at enhancing Levels 1 and 2. I asked him how he maximizes reaction and learning. Here is what he sent to me,

> In responding to your question of creating interest, I convey that because of my own interest. As you know, I'm one who reads, listens and views material on a continual basis. That "keeps the flame lit" and that transfers to the magic of enthusiasm. I continually hear of teachers who change students' lives by their deep interest and enthusiasm for their subject or for learning itself. Enthusiasm is the number one chapter of the Dale Carnegie Sales Course textbooks. When I teach or train, I initially try to create interest by how I present myself to the group. I move, look in the eye, gesture in a number of ways, with an outcome of wanting them to come along with me. I ask questions to initiate discussion—anything to "feel" that they are with me and we are moving on a path where learning is high. I look for indicators, while on my feet, that indicate concentration and belief. For instance, in leadership training, many relate it to position and not to personal influence. My point is that influence, and therefore leadership, is something that can be learned. The communi-

cator must be tuned in to make sure that connection is established and is continuing to build. I love to look people in the eye
and let them see my passion, and let them know that this can
benefit them. That's why "in it for me" philosophy creates in
them an even greater desire to absorb (Level 2) and put into
practice (Level 3). Finally, I speak with authority. Jesus was said
to speak with authority and not like one of the teachers of the
law. Ultimately, the wise person hears and applies, the foolish
builder only hears.

Dale and other many other professionals have learned not to wait until
after a training program or course is completed to assess how it is being
received. Effective trainers are able to assess continually during training and make adjustments as needed. Reaction sheets are a standard
way to evaluate reaction after the fact. If designed properly, they can
tell you how well a program was received, how participants found the
facility and atmosphere, and to what degree they believe the information presented will be useful to them on the job. This is basically a
"customer satisfaction" measure. They need to be developed prior to
training to ensure that the right content and methods are built into it.

Finally, my dad and I are big believers in the *PIE approach*—practical, interactive, and enjoyable. Near as I can tell, he made it up, although it has not achieved the same notoriety as his four levels has.

LEVEL 2: LEARNING

My other good friend, who works as a training director for the city of
Indianapolis, is John Galloway. John believes that much can be put
into the design of training programs to increase the likelihood that
good learning will take place. Quite logically, if this does not occur, it
is unreasonable to expect employees to transfer *what they did not learn*
to new behaviors on the job.

John is more a "bullet" kind of guy, while Dale is more a "paragraph"
kind of guy. Here is a list of suggestions, many courtesy of John, that I
suggest will enhance Level 2 learning:

- Have preclass discussions with bosses to develop clear expecta-
  tions for learning and postclass on-the-job implementation.
- Include line-of-business leaders and executives as trainers.
- Include presentations of best practices by front-line employees.

- Announce at the beginning of class that participants will be tested for knowledge, and skills will be practiced and critiqued in class.
- Announce at the beginning of class that participants will be expected to report learnings and applications to their teams following training.
- Use demonstrations of new behaviors, either live or via video-tape.
- Include relevant role-playing.
- Use visuals, anecdotes, stories, and illustrations where appropriate.
- Make effective use of e-learning.

PRINCIPLES OF ADULT LEARNING

Denise and I enjoy watching international news on television together. We especially like to discuss and debate what is presented. Sometimes, however, we run into a problem. Denise is a very strong auditory learner, and I am very visual. While the news is on, she almost exclusively *listens* to what the newscasters are saying, while I tend to *read* the text rolling across the bottom of the screen. Unfortunately, one usually has nothing to do with the other. She'll hear something interesting and say, "What do you think about that?" and I won't know what she is talking about. I will say, "Wow. Can you believe that?" to which she will reply, "I never saw it."

Numerous books and articles on the market not only do a great job of detailing methods to enhance learning, but also explain and apply the concepts of adult learning. Therefore, I will be brief here. My main point is to be aware of the different ways adults learn (hearing, seeing, doing, among others) and integrate corresponding methods in your training. We probably all know that lectures are not the most effective method to maximize learning. The above-mentioned suggestions cover a variety of learning styles.

EVALUATING LEARNING

Trainers need to be able to assess to what degree learning has occurred. Common and effective ways include competency pen and paper tests, performance tests, surveys from trainees and their supervisors, interviews, and combinations of these.

PART TWO—A FINAL WORD

I suggest you write down ideas presented in this chapter and in the following chapters that you think will benefit your organization. Then, set up a lunch with some bright, trusted colleagues, either internal or external, and talk your ideas through with them. I always find that to be most helpful, as my colleagues always seem to help me decide which ideas might realistically be accepted and prove beneficial.

PART III

SOLUTIONS TO THE CHALLENGE

I often refer to a concept in Tom Peters' *In Search of Excellence** that *capturing the hearts and minds* of employees is critical to corporate success. Our leadership development program at First Indiana is built on that principle. Our belief and training focus on both components. Capturing the *minds* of employees involves training, teaching, and coaching them to do their jobs. They have to know cognitively (i.e., minds) what the overall strategy of the organization is, how their area contributes to that strategy, and specifically what is expected of them. They learn much of this through on-the-job feedback and coaching from coworkers as well as from their supervisor. We believe that people have to be clear about those expectations and be given the resources, skills, and systems to accomplish their tasks.

Capturing their *hearts* is a whole different matter. This has everything to do with support, encouragement, and motivation. The mindset exists that "Employees shouldn't need that stuff. Children do, but

---

*Tom Peters and Robert Waterman, *In Search of Excellence* (Warner Books, 1982).

employees are adults and should be internally motivated. It should be enough for them to do a good job." For some, that may be true. Certainly many adults have strong internal motivation. However, research and common observation tells us that for a department or organization to perform successfully, a certain amount of support is required. This can come in the form of competitive salary, benefits, written notes of appreciation, showing an interest in the lives of employees, etc. Attending to both the hearts and minds of employees and managers is often the difference between achieving commitment over mere compliance.

ATTACKING THE CHALLENGE

This is the heart of the book: *How to get leaders and employees to transfer what they have learned into meaningful on-the-job behavior.* The key to achieving this, and ultimately training and organizational success, depends on the balance of two forces, *support* and *accountability*. Many individual trainers and training managers, as well as line managers, put a great deal of time, effort, and resources into actual training, but fail to put that same kind of effort into making sure trainees apply what they learn.

Remember the balanced scorecard training example I used earlier? Let's dig into it a little deeper. Let's say I conducted a two-day workshop with a group of about thirty managers on how to develop and implement balanced scorecards to improve profitability. Let's also say I did a pretty good job of it, including success with Levels 1 and 2. Let's also say that this is a sound and effective initiative (which it is). Now, we are at the doorstep of our challenge. *To what degree will they apply what they learned?* I submit to you that the participants separated themselves into three groups—the *Reachers*, the *Responders*, and the *Resisters*.

The light of insight and wisdom will go on for the *Reachers*. Thankfully, we have many Reachers at First Indiana. Marilyn Jones, a manager in our Retail area, is one of them. During training, Marilyn sat in the front row, asked questions, and volunteered for exercises and role-plays. Afterwards, she saw the benefits of the program for the bank, for their customers, for their employees, and for herself. As a result of seeing this value, she took what she learned and *proactively* went forth and applied it. She utilized team members in all phases of implementation and used organization and followup skills to ensure that the initiative continued. If all leaders were Reachers, there would be no need for this book. But, alas, they are not.

The next group is the *Responders*. We have a bunch of them at our bank, and are glad we do. Charlie Muggins (fictitious name) is a manager in our Commercial division. Charlie is a good guy and faithfully attended all twelve hours of the training. He asked some questions, and thoughtfully responded when asked for his input. After training, Charlie went back to his office to find work had stacked up. He had intended to finish his plan to develop and implement his balanced scorecard, but set it aside to get to more pressing matters. Fortunately, I built followup steps into the plan to help Charlie actually get it done. He might not have got it done on his own, but he did so with some encouragement and support. Chapter 6 is for helping you work with people like Charlie.

Nancy Jenkins is a member of the third group, the *Resisters*. Fortunately, there is no one by the name of Nancy Jenkins at First Indiana, but while she is fictitious, every organization has people with her traits. Nancy is not a bad person. She does, however, lead ineffectively. She was only able to attend eight of the twelve hours of training, and when she was there, she sat in the back with Eric Cravitz, another Resister. They chatted back and forth, and more than once I had to redirect their attention to the workshop. Nancy is one who thinks it is her job to scrutinize and analyze any new venture in terms of why it won't work. The glass tends to be half empty for Nancy, and the BSC Course was no exception. Although most of the time she sat in silence, occasionally she did challenge the usefulness of the whole initiative. Just for the record, I encourage disagreement and the expression of concerns and challenges. However, there is a distinction between genuine concerns and just plain resisting new ideas. Nancy is the latter. After training, Nancy took her workbook, put it on her bookshelf, and went back to her everyday work.

Chapter 6 will not suffice for the Nancys of the world, which is why there is a Chapter 7. Marilyn successfully implemented a new system by deliberately changing behavior. Charlie needed some consistent support to get it done, and Nancy needed both support and accountability. To be effective with all types of employees, you need to know how and to what degree you need to balance support and accountability.

You have three groups where you work, as well. You know members of each. You need to know how to get the most out of them.

Chapter 6

Support

I conducted the inaugural meeting of the First Indiana Book Club a month or so ago. First Indiana University is going to hold these periodically over the lunch hour to provide an opportunity for associates at all levels to grow professionally. The book we chose to be our first was *Fish!* by Stephen C. Lundin. Prior to each of the four hour-long sessions, I e-mailed the reading assignment to attendees along with questions to ponder. As with the senior team book review of Kaplan and Norton's *Strategy-Focused Organization*, these were questions not only to check for understanding but to challenge the readers personally. One of the participants was Erin Willem from our Information Technology department. One of the questions we discussed was "How do you keep from going to seed in your job?" "Going to seed," according to *Fish!*, means to become stale and complacent.

Erin had plenty to say about that. "I have been with the bank for only three months, but already I love it. My supervisor, Jay Vachon, provides me with great training on how to do my job [i.e., capturing the mind]. But this kind of experience [book club] really makes me want to come to work in the morning. If I was not motivated in my work and professionally challenged and encouraged, I would be in danger of going to seed—just going through the motions without really caring. Actually, I would probably leave the organization if that were the case."

THE MANY FACES OF SUPPORT

Many managers underestimate the force and impact of support. Support is a rather generic word, so let's look at its many faces. Support can come in the shape of formal and informal recognition. We formally recognize our top performers through nomination-based programs such as "Player of the Quarter" and "Best of the Best." We also have a "Star Night," which is a big, year-end celebration for our top sales and service associates. Recognition, of course, can also be informal. A culture that encourages not only manager-to-employee but also employee-to-employee recognition almost always increases productivity and morale. Support can also be expressed by just *showing an interest* in one another. When I come back from a workshop and one of our managers asks, "Hey, what did you learn that you can teach us?", it gives me the feeling that who I am and what I know is valued. Another good way that support is manifested is through incentives. Linking critical job-specific behaviors and results with incentives is an important example of support.

One of the most effective ways of showing support is by *showcasing best practices* and subsequent results. I am constantly on the prowl to find living examples of leaders and other associates who have applied new behaviors and achieved dramatic results. Fortunately, I have enough influence regarding meeting agendas that I can usually find a good place to include them. Believe me, the audience—usually upper and middle managers—are much more impressed with a testimonial from their peers than they are with words of praise or instruction from me. During our high-level Policy and Planning Committee meeting, for instance, I invited Erin from IT to talk with our senior team.

Early in World War II, Winston Churchill sent this message to Franklin D. Roosevelt: "Give us the tools and we will finish the job." The situation in business and industry is similar. Employees at all levels want the resources they need to do their jobs. They need the *proper conditions, systems, and resources* to do their jobs. Job success would mean including supplies, hardware and software, freedom from harassment, and a comfortable work environment. Finally, support includes *opportunity for growth and advancement.* Many studies on why people stay in jobs conclude that this is the number one reason.

Support most often comes from the outside, but don't ignore the powerful force of *internal support.* People are capable of generating a great deal of support for themselves. I try to find out how my direct reports build support into their own lives, then I encourage them to call on that support when things get stressed.

Some of you may be saying, "Well, that was interesting reading, but it wasn't anything I haven't already heard." That may be. But one of my motives is to spur you to implement (Level 3) some of these methods instead of just being familiar with them (Level 2).

THE PAPER CLIP GUY

One of the best illustrations of the words "support in action" is the Microsoft Paper Clip Guy (he looks male to me) who has been helping me to write this book. My computer-wise daughter Kara informed me that his name is Clippet. He just twitched when I typed his name and appeared to be rather pleased. I really do believe he is the epitome of support. When I started Chapter 1, he asked me, "It looks like you are typing a letter. Would you like some help?" How's that for support? It was the middle of the night and no one else was up except Clippet. He is constantly there to offer me suggestions, unless I ask him to leave, which he does without a whimper. He asks me if I would like to save something, concerned that I might lose edits that I have made. He maintains good eye contact, stays off to the side so he is never in the way, helps me with spelling, and even waves to attract my attention when he thinks I am really doing something wrong. But he never forces his opinions on me. He also makes me laugh with some of his shenanigans. Like everyone, however, he isn't perfect. During my writing of Chapter 3, I was really stuck with a sentence structure question. I looked over to him for help and he was scratching his head—cross my heart.

Let's look at these sources of support one at a time and consider some specific ways to bring them to life. These will be things that you can practice with all employees in your organization, and can build into *leadership development training* so that all managers can support training. This will increase the likelihood of a successful journey from Level 2 to Level 3 to Level 4.

FORMAL AND INFORMAL RECOGNITION

My guess is that most of you have pretty good recognition programs. They are not too difficult to develop and are usually big hits. We make sure that those recognized always display desired behaviors linked to tangible results or impact and that the recognition events are high profile. We just concluded a formal recognition campaign, Race to Recognition, that I would like to tell you about because it was a success, was relatively inexpensive, and involved associates at all levels recognizing each other. The idea came from a colleague of mine, though my assistant added a few twists. First, we created some blank one dollar checks and gave ten to each associate in the bank. Along with the checks, we had managers explain the program by telling their direct reports that this was a recognition program for everybody. Anybody could sign a check and present it to anyone else. They went on to explain the type of behaviors that we wanted to emphasize and, thus, be used as criteria for doling out the money. We ran the campaign for four weeks. At the end, we held auctions at different sites where associates could bid on and purchase items with their money. The most prized auction items were the ones that members of the senior team donated. They included symphony tickets, a Ping putter, a poolside cook-out, baseball cards, and autographed sports memorabilia.

I can guarantee that a lot of your colleagues in other organizations have equally good or better ideas for formal events and programs. Ask them. They are usually more than glad to share them.

Informal recognition is sometimes even more powerful. It cannot, however, be directed or required. Most of it comes from a corporate culture of care and the belief in the value of individual leaders. It recognizes and encourages their direct reports. Do what you can to enhance that atmosphere. A major skill that we reinforce continually to our leaders is the skill of giving positive feedback. As many of you do, we try to make sure that whenever praise is given, *details of why* we think the person or group did a good job are included. After all, if someone doesn't know exactly what they did to get praise, how will they know what continue?

SHOWING AN INTEREST

This one is easy, simple, yet often ignored. I will offer no special tactics or trade secrets here. It is merely making an effort to show that you care about another individual's personal and professional life. I try to keep close track of what my trainers are doing so I can encourage them and offer help if needed. If someone is having a particular challenging day, I look for a down minute, sit by their desk, and ask them how it's going. If they went away with their family for a long weekend, I will ask them how things went when they return. I do know of managers who make a habit walking around and greeting each person in their department every morning. They offer a genuine good morning and ask them if they are facing any particular challenges. This is very natural for leaders who tend to be interpersonal. It is very unnatural for those who are not or believe that work is work and kind words are not necessary. With regard to specifically supporting training, teach managers to show an interest in what their direct reports have learned (Level 2) in training and what commitments they have made toward applying (Level 3) what they have learned. The set of skills we call *followup* comes into play here. If you are good at this, great. If not, I suggest you find a way to build these behaviors into your daily work.

LINKING PERFORMANCE TO INCENTIVES

An important way to support new behaviors is to reward them. This can either be done in a recognition campaign such as our Race to Recognition or with employees' performance standards. It is certainly linked to accountability, but also must be considered as support.

Our Retail Banking Division offers a case in point. Up until five years ago, our tellers (we call them Customer Service Representatives) basically carried out customer transactions and made sure their drawers balanced. Because of our 2000 strategic directive to serve as *trusted advisors*, their role had to evolve. They are now key relationship builders with customers, which includes some aspects of selling and making referrals. Our retail banking division offers many opportunities for them to earn extra money by making customer referrals to other areas of the bank and opening new accounts. The transition from a transaction-oriented role to a consultative sales role would have been a very difficult transition without those incentives. During that journey, we learned a lot about transferring learning to new behaviors and used a combination of many different aspects of support and accountability to pull it off. Our Human Resources Department has done a fine job with establishing methods to determine performance standards.

SHOWCASING SUCCESSES

I utilize this one as often as I can. Individuals and teams of employees present their methods and successes in front of peers and middle and upper management. This benefits everyone. The employee benefits by allowing senior leaders to witness their presence, their skills, and their results. It also gives them a good dose of confidence. Senior management benefits by seeing fresh talent. Other managers present learn new ways to increase productivity. And training leaders benefit by gaining some free, highly effective promotion of training programs and methods. Besides meetings, internal newspapers and intranet websites are also great places to showcase best practices and successes.

I met some wonderful professionals in India recently while speaking at the annual India Society for Training and Development conference in Calcutta. Venkata Sundaram was one of them. Venkata is the Senior HRD Manager for National Mineral Development Corporation. He shared with me the following methods they use to showcase successes.

Quality Circles—As you probably know, Quality Circles (QC) is a voluntary group activity to encourage employees (blue and white collar) to involve themselves in the organizational processes and to provide a platform for their creativity.

To encourage people to take part in this quality circle movement (Level 3), we have adopted a system of sponsoring the successful (Level 4) QC teams to the Chapter Conventions of Quality Circle Forum of India, which are held at different locations. Those who are successful and qualify in these conventions are considered for participation in the Regional and National Events. Participation in the conventions helps the employees interact with the QC team members from other organizations and a great deal of learning (Level 2) occurs.

National Competition for Young Managers—Young Managers in our organization are encouraged to participate in the "National Competition for Young Managers" organized every year on different themes by *All India Management Association, India*. The objective of the competition is to provide unique opportunities for young managers to demonstrate their knowledge, experience, creativity and leadership skills so as to prepare them for greater roles. Initial participation will be at the Regional Level and successful teams will go to the Grand Finale. Participation in these events helps our managers to understand the external world and to recognize the changes taking place around the world.

There is one word in the above quote that I would like to emphasize— *creativity*. I believe that a good dose of support is a necessary ingredient to bring out creativity in managers and employees. In addition to cultivating internal support systems, I have one final suggestion. It is important for these show-and-tell showcasing events to come across as professional. Make sure you work with those who are to present so that they are well rehearsed and confident. I was reminded of this lesson a few months ago, the hard way.

In our very large managers' meeting we call Indiana Group, I invited and persuaded a female associate to show the group a new balanced scorecard measure she developed. Prior to the meeting, we *sort of* practiced, and she said she would do all right. Well, during her three-minute talk, she lost her thoughts and turned to me and said, "Oh, Jim. I knew this would happen!" One hundred and fifty pairs of eyes looked at her with compassion and care, then turned to me as if to say, "How could you let this happen to her?" Fortunately, they understood her nervousness and the points she was making.

PROVIDING PROPER CONDITIONS, SYSTEMS, AND RESOURCES

The best thing you can do to support the new behaviors you are asking of people is to model them yourself. This sounds easy, but it would be worth your while occasionally to take an inventory of your own behaviors to ensure you are practicing what you preach. Time that you spend coaching managers to be role models is time well spent.

We use a triangle model that leads to success if our associates are reasonably strong in each area: associates should be *ready, able,* and *willing* to do their jobs. This means that they will clearly understand what is expected of them, have the skills and resources to carry out what is expected of them, and be willing to do the job. When we run into performance snags with individuals or groups, one or more of these three components is usually lacking. The one in discussion here—providing proper conditions, systems, and resources—has everything to do with employees being *able*. Trainers teach managers and supervisors to check periodically with their direct reports to close any gaps in any of these areas.

CREATING OPPORTUNITIES FOR GROWTH AND ADVANCEMENT

Envision University, which serves Envision Financial Corporation in Vancouver, British Columbia, Canada, offers a great model of a Career Development Center. They offer easy-to-access opportunities to any employee to become involved in their program. I spent some time with them in 2003, and will visit with them again later this year. Carol Hama, the dean of the university, believes that their program not only helps individuals get on the right career paths, but also has a positive impact on productivity and morale. Their basic belief, from very sound research, is that employees who are in jobs that maximize their skills, abilities, education, and passion will enjoy their work, be productive, and want to stay with that company. Envision's high productivity and low turnover demonstrate the truth of that statement. Envision University also realizes the importance of training and equipping managers to support those same ideals. This is another example of the need for a cooperative effort between a corporate university or training department and nontraining managers and supervisors within the corporation.

One final suggestion I offer is to include employee development in the job descriptions of managers at all levels.

HOW TO SUPPORT AREA MANAGERS

Start at the top. I am thankful that our Chairman knows the importance of support. Not every leader does. Members of our corporate university spend a lot of time conducting formal training and informal coaching sessions to reinforce the importance of support. One of the most important ways we, as trainers, can teach managers to support their employees is to support the managers. All of the principles and methods that are described in this chapter are things that we strive to do for our internal customers. Reinforce what they do well. Observe, offer feedback, and coach them on the things they do not do well.

WHAT YOU CAN DO TO OFFER STRONGER SUPPORT

I share the following list with you because there will likely be something on it that you will see and say, "Wow. That would work for us!" and you'd immediately know how to implement it. This is a list of support-related best practices that were sent to me from my group of international colleagues when asked the question "What methods have you found that facilitate the successful transfer of learning to behavior?"

- Include modeling and practice.
- Make sure people get a chance to use immediately what they have learned.
- Share the rationale for changes and new behaviors.
- Take care that managers observe and reinforce correct behaviors.
- Be sure upper management understands that new behaviors and subsequent success take a while to build.
- Ask senior managers to call or visit top performers to recognize them.
- Split courses into smaller parts to allow time for on-the-job application.
- Share the benefits of any new expectations.
- Conduct posttraining evaluations.
- Use learning assignments between training sessions.
- Use group implementation to create mutual support.
- Separate development training and expectations from performance ones.
- Offer merit awards.

FINAL THOUGHT

I will conclude this chapter with two suggestions. First, consider developing an entire initiative around the concept of engaging associates. Research continues to show that this is an extremely effective way of retaining your high performers. Second, if offering support in the ways described in this chapter is not natural for you, you will need to develop a deliberate plan to do so. It will require you to develop new habits. It might also be a good idea to share your plan with a colleague to establish some personal accountability for change. Speaking of accountability, on to Chapter 7.

Chapter 7

Accountability

We have a piano in our house. It isn't a real good one, but it seems to work OK. It spent a month or so sitting in our front entryway, where it didn't belong. Denise wanted it moved. In fact, she asked me to move it after two weeks. After two more weeks, we were driving in the car and she said to me, "That old piano is still in the entryway. I would like you to move it, please." It was a rather rainy day, so my mood was not the highest. "Where would you like me to put it?" was my rather curt reply. "Do I have to think of everything?" she replied, and then added, "Well, if you can't figure out what to do with it, I can envision myself with Abe Lincoln's axe to take it out piece by piece."

Thus I introduce you to the meaning of *accountability*. (Note that with certain forms of accountability, there may exist an element of threat.) None of her Chapter 6 supportive words during the past few weeks had any effect on me, at least not to the point where Level 3 behavior occurred (i.e., moving the piano). So, she resorted to a different method, accountability. The piano was moved in less than two hours.

In the introduction to Part Three, I talked about the three groups of managers who took the Balanced Scorecard course. Marilyn Jones, representing the *Reachers* group, saw the wisdom and benefit of the course and immediately applied it to her job. Charlie Muggins, distinguished member of the *Responders* group, developed and implemented his BSC with some consistent support. Nancy Jenkins, a *Resister*, needed something more. I don't want you to think that people always fall into one category. I, for one, tend to switch groups depending on the issue and circumstances. In the case of the malingering piano, I was obviously a Resister. This chapter is about the force of accountability and how, as trainers and managers, we need to utilize those methods to bring this about in ourselves and others.

HOLDING OURSELVES ACCOUNTABLE

It all starts here for two reasons. First, we must model what we expect from others. If we don't follow through on what we say we will do and perform in the new ways to which we have committed, we can surely not expect others to do so. Second, holding ourselves accountable for new behaviors will produce the positive results we are looking for.

Every Friday, I develop a weekly action plan for the next week. I include specific tasks I plan to accomplish, by when, and comments. I also keep track of when those tasks are completed. I send my action plan to my boss and my direct reports. This is an extremely effective way for me to remain accountable to do what I say I will do. My direct reports do the same. It is up to me to keep track of my commitments and make sure I get them done. I am more prone to the supportive side of things, so I have to work on accountability. If you want to make just one significant change in your accountability quest, I suggest this one.

USING BALANCED SCORECARDS FOR ACCOUNTABILITY

Guess what heads this list? The balanced scorecard. Chapter 4 detailed the *science* of building one. This chapter will describe the *art* of making the system work. Figure 2 is an example of a line-of-business scorecard from the Small Business Development area at (fictitious) Fourth National Bank. Please refer to it during the following discussion.

This scorecard is a more sophisticated version of the Training and Development scorecard presented in Chapter 4, with three differences. First, I included numbers that referenced specific strategies under *Strat.*

Figure 2.

Fourth National Bank

2004 Balanced Scorecard—Small Business Development

"Raise questions. Seek information. Make strategic decisions."

September 2004

Manager: Mary Wells

No.	Strat.	Category	Monthly Results				YID Results		
			Actual	Target	Status	Chng.	Actual	Target	Status
A		**Financial/Production Measures:**							
1	1a	Fee income	55,000	59,000	C	nc	450,000	550,000	C
2	1b	Commercial deposits	400,000	410,000	OT	–	430,000	400,000	OT
3	1c	Direct net income	500,000	200,000	ET	+	3,000,000	1,500,000	ET
4	2a	Number of RMs per support employee	4	4	OT	+			
5	2c	Operating expense	80,000	90,000	OT	–	850,000	800,000	OT
		Customer Measures:	Actual	Target	Status	Chng.	Actual	Target	Status
1	1a	Number new DD accounts	50	40	OT	+	380	450	C
2	1a	$ new DD accounts	6,500	8,000	C	+	37,000	49,000	C
3	3a	Inbound internal referrals	6	20	NH	–	75	150	NH

			Actual	Target	Status	Chng.	Actual	Target	Status
4	3a	Inbound referrals closed	8	10	OT	+	90	100	OT
5	3a	Customer referrals	4	5	C	new			
6	4a	New customer satisfaction	84%	97%	NH	–	90%	97%	C
		Internal Systems Measures:	**Actual**	**Target**	**Status**	**Chng.**	**Actual**	**Target**	**Status**
1	3b	Outbound referrals	25	20	OT	nc	192	180	OT
2	1a-c	Prospect contacts	25	45	NH	–	300	320	OT
3	1a-c	Customer contacts	45	25	ET	+	320	190	ET
4	1a-c	Number joint calls with manager	15	10	OT	new			
5	1a-c	Customer profile quality	75%	90%	NH	–	82%	90%	C
6	5a	Percent customer inquiry calls win 24 hrs	97%	98%	OT	+	90%	98%	C
7	5c	Customer impact errors	5	3	C	–	26	27	OT
		Learning & Growth Measures:	**Actual**	**Target**	**Status**	**Chng.**	**Actual**	**Target**	**Status**
1	3a	Internal needs assessments condot.	2	2	OT	nc	19	18	OT
2	1,6a	Trainee reaction scores	4.5	4.5	OT	+	4.2	4.5	C
3	1,6a	Percent trainee competency passed	90%	95%	C	–	94%	95%	OT
4	7a	Employee loyalty scores	4.5	4.3	OT	nc	4.5	4.3	OT

Figure 2. (*continued*)

No.	Strat.	Category	Monthly Results				YTD Results		
		Learning & Growth Measures:	Actual	Target	Status	Chng.	Actual	Target	Status
5	7b	Associate turnover	0%	2%	OT	nc	12%	15%	OT
6	7a-b	Training plans on target	75%	100%	NH	new			

Exceeds Target	=ET
On Target	=OT
Caution	=C
Needs Help	=NH

Better	+
No Change	nc
Worse	–
New Measure This Month	new

Free Income

Outbound Referrals

Second, I included year-to-date results in addition to monthly ones. Third, I included two graphs along the right side. The scorecard gives you a snapshot of what is happening at a given moment in time, and the graphs show a trend. Our managers choose graphs that show significant trends they want to emphasize.

This concept is critical to the success of our training program: *training measures are included throughout this scorecard.* It is one thing to have training measures within a Training and Development BSC; it is quite another to have been able to persuade nontraining managers to include them in theirs. Also note that all four levels for evaluating training effectiveness are present:

- Trainee reaction scores (under *Learning and Growth*)—Level 1
- Percent trainee competency passed (under *Learning and Growth*)—Level 2
- Training plans on target (under *Learning and Growth*)—Level 2
- Percent customer inquiry calls (returned) within 24 hrs (under *Internal Systems*)—Level 3
- Number of joint calls with managers (under *Internal Systems*)—Level 3
- Prospect and customer contacts (under *Internal Systems*)—Level 3
- Customer referrals (under *Customer*)—Level 4
- Commercial deposits (under *Financial*)—Level 4
- Fee income (under *Financial*)—Level 4

Whether or not you use this system, my point is that it is imperative to get line-of-business managers to measure training-related activities and be able to link them to results.

To review, I will present a cause-and-effect example from this scorecard to illustrate how Mary Wells, the manager, is to answer the question "How do you plan to increase Fee Income in the next three months?" Let's see if she understands the link between training and results, and the transfer of learning to behavior:

Mary: "Well, first I have to make sure my people are equipped with the right understanding and skills to generate more fee income. This is accomplished through training. You see the measures here (Trainee reaction scores and Percent trainee competency passed under *Learning and Growth*)? They indicate to me the degree to which my people find the training useful and enjoyable and actually learn what they are supposed to learn. Apparently they do like it (high reaction scores), but we need to find out how to increase their learning (subtarget competency scores). Once we do that, I will carefully monitor these two measures (Number of joint calls and Customer profile quality under *Internal Systems*). These skills are what they are being trained to do, and I want to make sure that they are applying that knowledge to their everyday work. When those skills maintain their targets, we can expect an increase in these measures in the *Customer* dimension (pointing to Number of and $ new DD accounts), which will in turn lead to a nice increase in fee income (under *Financial*)."

Hurray! She got it!! It is easy to tell how this type of system and discussion promotes accountability. It contains objective data that can be tracked and analyzed, and a plan that can be evaluated.

THE ART OF APPLYING BALANCED SCORECARDS

Following are some suggestions that will help you drive a system like this from development to successful execution.

1. Form a project team to develop drafts of Strategy Maps (see Kaplan and Norton's book for examples) and Balanced Scorecards. Then solicit comments from executive leaders to modify and finalize them. Work hard to achieve executive involvement and ownership.

2. Do *not* immediately link scorecard performance to incentives. This will invariably cause managers to cherry-pick measures that they know will reach or exceed targets. Make sure the message is clear that the purpose is to improve area performance. You might consider linking them to pay much later in the process.

3. Have the project team (or you!) review their development all along the way. Offer encouragement and suggestions where needed.

4. Enlist leaders at all levels to use their scorecards with their people to explain strategy and to measure how well it is being executed. Actively involve them in modifying and improving measures on an ongoing basis. Be sure all employees in an area see how their individual jobs contribute to success in each category.

5. Facilitate the cross-functional use of balanced scorecards. Do what you can to make sure they are used to educate and hold each other accountable, because most outcome measures require cross-function cooperation to improve.

6. Use the scorecards to provide information to senior executives. Do whatever you can to enlist those executives to ask BSC questions of their direct reports.

7. Showcase successes by having managers like Mary Wells show and tell what they have done. It is a great way to set an example that others can follow.

8. Devise a process whereby modifications are immediately made for every scorecard after any major change in strategy.

SMALLER-SCALE ACCOUNTABILITY METHODS

There are some really good ways to build in accountability *prior* to training. First, develop *preprogram contracts*. This process involves communicating with line-of-business managers or area leaders the importance of their role in their trainees' transfer of learning to behavior. Then reach and formalize agreements on what specific behaviors both training leaders and area leaders will perform to drive success. Followup is of obvious importance if this process is to be successful. Second, *performance objectives*, along with learning objectives, should be set. These should be actionable and observable. Third, insist that *management performance goals* include behaviors that support training and transfer. Finally, let employees know *prior to training* that they will be called on to make a report to their team or to an executive. That really helps to increase their attention, which will increase the likelihood of learning and on-the-job application.

Other suggestions for increasing accountability have been offered to me by my colleagues in the field. Here is a list of some of them, along with the ones I use:

1. *Conduct phone conferences.* This is especially good when dealing with people in remote locations. Let them know what will be discussed and what they will be expected to report on. Most managers don't want to say in front of their peers, "Well, I didn't get it done." Set *specific* commitments at the end of each call.

2. *Conduct regular meetings to set daily, weekly, and/or monthly goals.* I conduct a standing Friday morning meeting with our entire senior team from 8:30 to 9:00. The meeting consists of addressing a

high-level topic (e.g., increasing referrals, cutting costs, improving morale, and so forth) and generating *specific* (there's that word again) commitments—commitments that are observable, measurable, and time sensitive. The following week, we debrief those commitments and either move on to a new topic or continue with modified commitments for the next week. Often Marni will lead the meeting. Involvement and attention are greater than when I do it (obviously the difference between a chairman and a corporate training director). Similar meetings are held throughout the bank.

3. *Increase accountability through observation, feedback, and coaching.* Many of our scorecards have these measures under **Internal Systems.** It's true that this can be somewhat invasive; few employees like to be observed. But if it is explained that this is a way of caring, it can be done in a positive way. This is how I explain the rationale to people. "Every professional golfer has a coach. Do you think the coach tells and shows them how to improve their swing, then turns his back when they try it? Of course not. Only when the coach observes what they do and don't do (transferring learning to behavior) can he really be helpful." I believe the same principle applies when we correct anyone. A suggestion might be interpreted as criticism and resentment might occur.

4. *Conduct interviews with employees with whom you are conducting performance coaching.* Prior to a session, make sure you and the employee are both clear about what the employee is working on (Level 3). Let's say George is working on improving his customer profiling skills. When you meet, first ask him to *describe* what they did in a particular profiling session, then to *show* you his profile form. Do this respectfully and you can really see how well he is practicing the skills. It is of the utmost importance to use this followup method *very soon after training has been concluded* to create immediate reinforcement for new behaviors.

5. *Use a partner or mentor approach.* This is a good way to increase accountability. This works because there is a particular person who cares about your improvement in a particular area, and will meet with you on a regular basis or as requested. Most of us know how effective it is to have an accountability partner when it comes to things like exercising or dieting.

6. *Inspect documents to see if people have applied what they learned.* This is particularly appropriate with some sort of regulatory requirement, such as the Sarbanes-Oxley Act, in which the failure

to transfer learning to behavior can have serious consequences. Let employees know that you are going to do this, your rationale for it, and how you will work with them to improve.

7. *Initiate a certification process to enhance accountability.* As an example, Marianne Blackwell, in charge of our Consumer Finance training, requires three things for a home equity closer to become certified:

   a. course attendance

   b. 80 percent or higher on course quizzes

   c. a group of closing packages free of audit exceptions

   Thus, they must not merely prove knowledge, but also demonstrate application.

8. *Link incentives to the behavior and subsequent desired results.* This is very important, and you may be wasting your time if this isn't taken care of right from the start.

TOOLS FOR PROMOTING ACCOUNTABILITY

Most organizations solicit some sort of customer survey information either from their efforts or from a third party. At First Indiana, we do both. This data provides an important measure for many of our balanced scorecards under the **Customer Measures** category. This data also provides an excellent opportunity for accountability. Unfortunately, many managers of sales areas discount this valuable source of information, usually when the measures are lower than they'd like. "I don't believe a sample that small accurately reflects the opinions of our customers." "We don't believe third-party data nearly as much as we believe our own, since we know our customers so well." "If our customers were less than satisfied, I would be the first to know." As training leaders, try to push past this resistance and persuade executives to implement some sort of accountability to customer input.

Similarly, I strongly suggest you conduct regular *employee surveys.* We send one out electronically three times a year. We use the questions the Gallup Organization developed, the "Twelve Determinants of Employee Loyalty." Those particular questions seem to cover all or most of the cultural ingredients we are trying to build. Results are divided by department and sent to subsequent managers. Managers then meet with their staffs to select several issues to work on as a department and decide how they will do it. This provides an excellent accountability process to work on culture and leadership weaknesses.

Many leaders keep a *coaching journal.* This is a tool in which the trainer or manager writes down what is going well and what isn't in his or her coaching. It also includes the commitments that participants make to each other.

Here is a summary of the steps we use in the process to link Level 2 and Level 3 assessments to learning objectives. It is typically administered ninety days after course completion.

    A. **Learning Objective**: To be able to complete the closing packet of an auto loan within thirty minutes with no errors.

    B. **Level 2 Assessment**:

        1. Write out the steps that you would take to complete the packet.

        2. List and describe the six most common errors to watch out for.

    C. **Level 3 Assessment**: To what degree have you been able to apply the principles and methods of completing an auto loan closing packet?

        1. Completely.

        2. To a large degree, but I still have a few problems with it.

        3. To a large degree, but mostly from the lack of actually doing them.

        4. Not too well, since I keep making mistakes.

        5. Not too well, since it takes me too long.

        6. None, since I haven't had any opportunity to work on any.

We not only have the trainee complete a longer version of the above, but also have the supervisor do the same. This information is then used for improving training (if Level 2 scores are low) or coaching (if Level 3 scores are low).

A FINAL THOUGHT

Look for an overall trend in your organization that might indicate a general weakness in this area. This is very common, and keeps many good companies from becoming superior. If you find such a trend, talk with your senior executives about your insights, and consider developing a course for all managers and supervisors, complete with accountability for change.

Chapter 8

The Glue to Hold It All Together

My favorite way to fish is to put on chest waders, waterproof nylon overalls, and walk in cold streams and fish for trout. It is great fun unless they leak. I also like to fish out of my fiberglass canoe. It is also great fun unless it leaks or overturns. The year 2004 has been hard for fishing up to this point because I have suffered from ice cold water on my legs (leaky waders) and soggy shoes (leaky canoe). Fortunately, someone invented glue that can fix both. I just came in the house from fixing my waders and now I have this wonder-glue sitting in front of me as I write. This is not just ordinary white glue. This is special glue—so special that it comes in two separate tubes that must be mixed together. One tube is purple and says "Part A—Resin." The other comes in a red tube and says "Part B—Catalyst." The resin is apparently the foundation of the glue. The catalyst serves as the chemical accelerant and the stimulus that causes the resin to become glue. The directions, which incidentally I read, say that the two parts must be mixed together in equal parts *or it won't work*. And the last thing I want is to go out fishing and suffer through more leakage.

You may be wondering where I'm going with this. If you suspect that

I am offering a metaphor for *support* and *accountability*, you'd be incorrect. Obviously, I believe an organization needs a balance of both to maximize training effectiveness and productivity; this chapter is about two additional elements that will reinforce all of the principles and methods up to this point. I have alluded to them in previous chapters, but I now want to highlight them in this final chapter of Part Three.

Let's put the twin elephants right on the table. The *resin* is a metaphor for *the feedback loop* among training leaders, participants, and their mangers. The *catalyst* represents the ongoing, positive *business relationship* between training staff and senior executives. Here is why this is so important. If you have spent a lot of time, money, and energy working on the five prerequisites to training success and have a good balance of support and accountability, you certainly don't want to lose the great effect you are going to get by not pushing all the way through to the finish.

THE RESIN—FEEDBACK LOOP

Ultimate success starts with a good understanding of what I mean by feedback loop, and with whom it needs to occur. The feedback loop is the ongoing sharing of information, both objective and subjective, among all stakeholders. In the case of training, I'm talking about the following relationships:

- Training leaders and training participants
- Training leaders and training participants' managers
- Training participants and training participants' managers

The loop is critical to keeping everyone informed and involved. Feedback should be given in both directions in each of the above relationships. Feedback, just like learning methods, is best when it takes on multiple forms. Employee and customer surveys are sources of excellent feedback data. So are metrics that have been fashioned from learning objectives and desired outcomes. One of my favorites is a lunchtime discussion about "How do you think things are going?"

What follows is a summary of the on-boarding process that I developed for our branch managers last year. This template came from an Indianapolis colleague of mine. Its purpose is to link branch managers and their new associates during the first twelve months of their employment. The process focuses on *performance* and *engagement* and ensures that engagement and feedback occur regularly to maximize performance.

Prehire:
Recruitment/Selection

- Job discussion
- Structured interviews
- Selection tools

Supervision prepares for associate's arrival with on-board (OB) checklist

Assignment of job coach and peer partner

Office set-up

Supervisor leads OB meeting with staff in preparation of new associate's arrival

Week 1:
Associate attends New Associate Orientation

Associate attends job-related training

Supervisor/Associate Key Conversation #1

- Culture and strategy
- One-month expectations and commitments
- Department policies
- Motivation

Staff welcomes associate

HR forms filled out and turned in

Supervisor reviews OB checklist with job coach and peer partner

Months 1–2:
Supervisor/Associate Key Conversation #2

- Followup to one-month expectations and commitments
- Debrief training
- How are things going? What can I do to help? (throughout)
- Expectations and commitments

Months 3–5:

On-board interview between executive and new associate

Supervisor/Associate Key Conversation #3

- 90-day review
- Expectations and commitments

Months 6–9:

Supervisor/Associate Key Conversation #4

- Conduct Associate Needs Assessment
- Career discussion and guidance
- Expectations and commitments

Months 10–12:

Supervisor/Associate Key Conversation #5

- Yearly performance review
- Expectations and commitments

It goes without saying that feedback is of little use unless it is used to make improvements. But, I guess I said it anyway. My strong suggestion is that each of you develop a formal system of utilizing feedback by (a) determining root causes of any measures or reports that are substandard, (b) generating observable commitments based on the root causes, and (c) following up on all commitments.

THE CATALYST—MAINTAINING STRONG BUSINESS RELATIONSHIPS

I studied to be a game warden in my undergraduate days at the University of Wisconsin. Between my sophomore and junior years, I spent the summer in northern Wisconsin at a place called the Clam Lake Field Station. There we were taught six weeks' worth of wildlife management, forestry, and soil conservation. Forestry was the last of the three units, and I was feeling a little anxious to get home. That extra energy, unfortunately, led to a personal lapse in my good judgment. If I recall correctly, my friend Dave Rose and I caught and put some live fish in a barrel that our professor, Dr. Girrard, was using to collect rain water for some type of experiment. Well, whatever "strong collegial relationship" I had with Dr. Girrard apparently went south when he found the fish.

And here's how I found out. The next day, Dr. Girrard decided to take a group of four of us "timber cruising." Timber cruising is when you walk through the woods, and draw a map of all of the trees in a given area, including size and type. We headed off in his truck, and soon found ourselves traveling down "the road less traveled," an old logging road lined on both sides with thick brambles, thorny pricker bushes, and huge trees. He was apparently looking for a good place to drop us off. After we had traveled about two miles down the road, a huge black bear suddenly appeared and slowly ambled across the logging road about a quarter of a mile in front of us. No one said a word, as we hoped Dr. Girrard hadn't seen it. But he had. As we approached the exact spot where the bear had disappeared into the woods, he stopped the truck and said, "Smith and Hogus, you go that way and cruise that area (pointing to the way the bear had come), and Kirkpatrick and Rose, you two go that way (pointing to the way the bear had gone). I'll be back in four hours to pick you up."

I have not played practical jokes on professors or bosses since then. I do spend time cultivating relationships with senior managers because they remain the key to training success and improved productivity. There are lots of ways to do this. Fortunately for me, I like all of the senior leaders at First Indiana, so it is easy for me to want to work at our relationships. I try to spend time finding out how they are doing and if there are any issues that my department can help them with. I try to send them information on how training is benefitting them. Not only am I getting to know them, but I am also hoping that they solidify their belief about one particular point: Although many companies have the same technology, sales methods, strategies, service approaches, and hiring practices, *we differentiate ourselves by our people*. I want them to know that when all is said and done, our people are our competitive advantage, and we all need to nurture those relationships as much as possible.

My suggestion here is simple. Invest time in getting together both formally and informally with your senior executives. Educate them, learn from them, encourage them, and solicit their active involvement in training and coaching. It will pay high dividends.

First Indiana Bank's vision states that we are to serve the Central Indiana community as "trusted advisors" and develop "strong partnerships" with coworkers. We accomplish this by utilizing the basic strategy of *discovery*, *delivery*, and *dialogue* with our customers and partners. We believe that to execute these goals, internal partnerships must mirror the same kind of trust and collaboration that we strive for with our customers. The following examples highlight three training and development specialists at First Indiana, and how each implements these beliefs. All three strongly believe that their jobs as trainers are not done until Levels 3 and 4 are realized.

NANCY WRIGHT, MANAGER OF ASSOCIATE DEVELOPMENT

Nancy is an integral part of First Indiana University (FIU). She designs and delivers training programs to associates of all levels and in all areas of the bank. She delivers standard half-, full-, and two-day classes in both sales and service. She is also frequently called upon to customize classes and exemplifies FIU's business consulting model. Nancy believes strongly in excelling at Level 1 to set the stage for Levels 2 through 4. She takes great care in creating an inviting atmosphere including food and drink, tablecloths, flowers, and bright outside lighting, as well as detailed content preparation.

Not surprisingly, Nancy also works hard at Level 2. She wants her participants to understand and *find personal relevance* in what they are learning. She uses a balanced combination of videotapes, breakout groups, illustrations, workshops, role plays, frequent interaction, contagious enthusiasm, and pre- and postcompetency tests. She excels at drawing in those who are not actively participating in the learning process. She continually checks for understanding and is good at reading people to tell if they don't understand. She also commands a lot of respect and credibility from training participants, as she has extensive line management experience herself.

Nancy is included in this case study not so much for all of the above, but because she works hard at the challenge of transferring learning to behavior. Here are the specific techniques she uses to increase the likelihood that participants will apply what they learn:

- Frequently asks, "How will you use this when you return to your job?"
- Involves executives and managers in the design and delivery of courses
- Formally and informally teaches supervisors and managers how to support training

- Develops close working relationships with executives
- Ends every session with a call to action, requiring participants to generate an action plan
- Follows up with managers to see how their direct reports are applying what they learned
- Observes associate and manager performance and offers relevant feedback and coaching
- *Believes* she is responsible for results

MARIANNE BLACKWELL, TECHNICAL TRAINER AND SKILLS COACH

Marnianne is the lead trainer for First Indiana's Consumer Finance Bank. She is also a great member of the FIU faculty. She carefully designs programs by attending to the question, "What will participants need to know how to do on the job?" She is a believer in the FIU philosophy of designing comprehensive training programs for associates in different jobs. Marianne is organized and deliberate in her training, but always manages to make it relevant and enjoyable for her participants. Marianne also believes that her job flows through Levels 3 and 4. She has developed a series of competency tests, and utilizes a lot of support and practical help to ensure that participants pass her tests.

Much of Marianne's training is system driven. She explains, "One of the ways I get associates to transfer what they have learned into job application is by making sure *their systems do not work unless they do it right.*" She has also developed a certification process that greatly enhances that transfer; class and program graduates must show her evidence of using what they learned in order to get certified. For example, if she is teaching a class on creating consumer loan closing packages, she will review several to see that they have been done properly. Marianne is currently working with line-of-business managers to help hold their associates accountable. She is excellent at preparing reports to managers on the progress of their trainees, both during and after training. Marianne is also very good at working in adjunct faculty. She notes, "When trainees' managers are involved in delivering the training, it seems to increase the likelihood that the trainees will apply what they learn."

TRACY HUNTER, HR MANAGER

First Indiana Bank's Human Resources Department is integral to the overall training and development of all associates. HR partners well with FIU, and offers courses and coaching specifically designed to enhance the new associate hiring process, associate performance, and associate relations. Tracy oversees the recruiting arm of First Indiana, and it is within this context that she makes a great contribution to the bank.

Tracy states, "I focus on instilling the importance of people's work in the context of helping our customers, the bank, and themselves. I always try to explain context and rationale for everything I expect my recruiters to do." She challenges them to look at the impact of their efforts. Tracy's approach epitomizes the balance of *support* and *accountability*. How she uses each is detailed below:

Support

Tracy does a good job of building strong alliances with managers. She discovers their performance and staffing needs, and not only works to integrate their requests in her training and initiatives, but keeps them well informed on progress. She supports her recruiters by developing and maintaining open communication among them. Several weeks ago, under a heavy work burden, they came to her and said, "We would like a quiet day to focus on this particular project." Tracy responded not only with understanding, but with practical help. She found them a private place to work, forwarded *their* phones to *her*, and made herself available all day for whatever questions they had. She regularly keeps them focused, so that they are not overwhelmed by too many different priorities. She also lets them work, after making sure they are on the right track, and she does that respectfully, according to coworkers.

When asked how she specifically provides support, Tracy's first response was, "I don't know." Rhonda, a coworker, answered for her, "It's your personality. You are friendly, approachable, you show people that you have their best interests at heart, and you don't let your moods (if you have any) affect the way you deal with people." She went on to say, "Your openness and genuineness is exemplary in everything you do—the way you greet people, your interest in work-life balance, and the way you serve as a consistent role model." Tracy finally acknowledged some of this by saying, "Well, I never want to roll my eyes when someone asks me a question." Some of Tracy's success comes from her consistent behavior. Another element is the kind of person she is. These things can't be taught, but we all like to have people like this in our organizations.

Accountability

Don't think for a moment that Tracy is a "soft" leader. Tracy believes in and practices holding people accountable. HR in general and Tracy specifically make sure that whatever initiatives they are recommending, they get "buy-in from the top." Tracy has close working relationships with all of upper management, and regularly solicits their active support in new ventures. As a case in point, HR is currently working closely with bank leaders to keep associate turnover to a minimum. Tracy is extensively involved in this effort. Getting senior executives to deem this a top priority, asking them to direct all managers to include monthly turnover data on their balanced scorecards, and following up with higher turnover areas are good examples. Tracy provides relevant turnover data to all managers and encourages executives to follow up with managers who need support and accountability in this area.

Tracy also holds her direct reports accountable. They know what is expected of them, and she coaches to those standards and expectations. If she has concerns, she will directly yet respectfully talk with her people until barriers are overcome and performance is on track.

Nancy, Marianne, and Tracy all do a good job of tracking projects, behaviors, and outcomes on their balanced scorecards. They regularly summarize, analyze, and report this data, and involve themselves in discussions to overcome obstacles and make improvements. As a result, associates are clear about their job expectations, capable of performing the tasks that will lead to those outcomes, empowered to bring forth their own ideas, and look forward to coming to work every day.

SUPPORTIVE MANAGEMENT

Submitted by: Donald L. Kirkpatrick, PhD

Following is an example written by Don of how a manager can apply the kind of glue that will greatly increase the likelihood of employees applying what they have learned.

Transferring On-The-Job Training to Improved Behavior

STRATEGIC CHALLENGE

Nearly all of the attention has been concentrated on the transfer of training from classroom, e-learning, or a blending of both. One of the most effective approaches to training takes place on a regular basis between managers and subordinates. We call this on-the-job training. This case study will discuss the important performance appraisal by the manager and the necessary followup coaching.

Most organizations of any size have a formal performance appraisal program. Some (only a few) of these organizations conduct training programs on how to appraise, how to conduct the performance appraisal interview, and how to get improved performance from the process. In fact, in most organizations, the emphasis is on providing information for salary considerations, potential for promotion (and for retention), and communicating this to the direct report with little opportunity for the direct report to participate. To use the process for improved performance, a different approach must be taken. It involves much participation by the direct report.

TRAINING INTERVENTION

An effective program should include the following steps:

1. *Clarify what is expected of the direct report.* This is one of the most important steps and often ignored. Often, the manager will appraise on what he or she thinks the direct report should be doing, and it is different than what the direct report thinks is expected. Unless they agree, the direct report will not accept the appraisal. This sometimes involves a participative interview in which both parties communicate their understanding and agreement is reached.

2. *Conduct the interview.* I suggest that the manager comes to the interview with his/her appraisal written in pencil and thereby subject to change. This suggestion will be a shock to most people who are responsible for the performance appraisal program. I suggest that the participation be approximately 50/50, with each person talking about half the time. Sometimes it will be 80/20 in favor of the manager if the direct report is reluctant to talk, or it might be 20/80 if the direct report is overly talkative. The important point is that each has a say and they agree on the appraisal.

TRANSFERRING LEARNING TO BEHAVIOR

3. *Develop a Performance Improvement Plan.* This step is neglected in most programs. Usually, the boss will offer suggestions on what the direct report should do to improve performance and conclude the interview with a sigh of relief that the unpleasant job is done. It should end with agreement on one area of performance to improve and a Performance Improvement Plan that specifies what both the direct report and the manager will do to be sure that improvement takes place.

Figure 3. Performance Improvement Plan

Employee: John Green
Boss: Tom Severson, Department Head
Date: October 1
Performance to Be Improved: Orienting and Training New Employees

Action to be taken	By whom	By when
1. Talk with Karen Taylor about her approach.	J. Green	October 15
2. Watch Karen Taylor when she orients and trains a new employee.	J. Green	The next time she does it
3. Provide a checklist to John for orienting new employees.	L. Jackson, Training Director	October 15
4. Attend new employee orientation meeting conducted by HR department.	J. Green	The next time it occurs
5. Decide on best time for new employees to come to the department.	J. Green and HR	By October 20
6. Attend a seminar on "How to Train New Employees."	J. Green	November 15 U. of Wisconsin
7. Read the following books: (list three) *Self Development for Supervisors and Managers*, Allhiser *No Nonsense Communication*, Kirkpatrick *The Supervisor and On-the-Job Training*, Broadwell	J. Green	By October 15 By November 10 By December 12
8. Observe John orienting and training a new employee.	L. Jackson, Training Director	The next time John trains a new employee
9. Talk with John's next three new employees.	T. Severson	One week after hire

Figure 4. Coaching on the Performance Improvement Plan

Name: John Green, Supervisor **Boss:** Tom Severson, Dept. Head
Date: October 1
Performance to Be Improved: Orienting and Training New Employees

The Performance Improvement Plan				Coaching Contact by Tom Severson	
Action to be taken	**By whom**	**By when**	**Followup**	**Notes**	
1. Talk with Karen about her approach.	J. Green	October 15	October 14 October 15	Made arrangements to talk to Karen tomorrow. Talked with Karen. Got some good ideas.	
2. Watch Karen when she orients and trains a new employee.	J. Green	The next time she does it	October 15 November 15	Karen plans to train a new employee on Nov. 13. John will observe. Karen trained a new employee and John watched. Felt it worthwhile.	
3. Provide a checklist for John for orienting and training new employees.	L. Jackson, Training Director	October 15	October 13 October 21 October 25	Checked with Larry on checklist. Is not ready yet. Promised by October 21. Checked with Larry again. List not quite done yet. Checklist completed and given to John.	
4. Attend new employee orientation meeting conducted by HR.	J. Green	The next time it is done	October 15 November 18	Checked with HR and found out it will be done Nov. 18. Asked John to attend. John attended and passed along suggestions to HR.	

98

Action to be taken	By whom	By when	Followup	Notes
5. Decide on best time for new employees to come to department.	J. Green working with HR	By October 20	October 19	Worked out the starting time for all new employees: 9 am on Monday instead of 7 am.
6. Attend a seminar on "How to Train New Employees."	J. Green	November 15	November 12 November 18	Discussed program schedule and details. Discussed program and benefits John received from it.
7. Read the following books: Allhiser's Kirkpatrick's Broadwell's	J. Green	October 15 November 10 December 12	October 3 October 14 October 31 November 5	Arranged to order 3 books for John. Learned that John has read half of Allhiser's book. Learned that John has read half of Kirkpatrick's and all of Allhiser's. Learned that John has finished first 2 books.
8. Observe John orienting and training a new employee.	L. Jackson	The next time John trains a new employee	October 20 November 20	Learned that John is schedule to hire a new employee on November 15. Received good feedback from Larry on John's training of new employee.
9. Talk with John's next three new employees.	T. Severson	One week after hire	November 25	Talked with Ralph Cador, John's new employee, about his start with the company. Generally felt good about orientation, but is still confused about benefits. Doesn't feel secure in job yet.

Figure 3 is an example of a plan where it was *jointly determined* that the direct report, John Green, agreed to do certain things and that the department head, Tom Severson, also agreed to do certain things. This is a Performance Improvement Plan that both have agreed to implement.

4. *Develop a coaching plan.* In many organizations that develop such a plan, the assumption is made that each party will carry out the plan. This is similar to training programs in which it is assumed that the trainee will apply learning to job behavior. Here is where the manager takes charge of seeing that the agreement is followed. He or she develops a Coaching Plan (Figure 4) that spells out what will be done and when to *be sure* that the Performance Improvement Plan is actually implemented.

OUTCOME

These four steps provide the basis and motivation for effective transfer of on-the-job training to improved behavior and better results. Trainers should be aware of on-the-job training as an important process to improve behavior and thereby results. In fact, they should be a part of the performance appraisal program. They should help to develop the forms and provide the training needed by managers to do an effective job.

PART THREE—A FINAL WORD

My dad is a golfer. Well, at least he likes to play golf. He has a favorite club that he calls a "chipper." He uses it quite often. It has gotten him out of many a tight spot. We all have a "chipper" in our bag of tricks to move training from delivery to results. My dad is aware of the fact that he has other clubs in his golf bag, and he uses different ones when the situation calls for something other than his beloved chipper.

Make sure you identify and use the other clubs in the bag of tricks that you use to drive training through to results. If you tend to be more into support, deliberately look for opportunities to use accountability, and vice versa, and teach your managers to do the same.

PART IV

BEST PRACTICES
CASE STUDIES

FROM JIM:

I do my most creative thinking while I am asleep. Many times the approach to a challenge or problem comes to me in a dream. Sometimes I remember it and sometimes I don't. Earlier this month, I was trying to determine what format to request for these Best Practices Case Studies. Nothing satisfactory came to me during my waking hours. That night, while sound asleep, I dreamt that I was awakened by a noise in our sun room. I crawled out of bed to find out who or what it was. As I neared the room, I could hear two soft male voices. I peaked around the corner into the sun room to see who had intruded our home. There I found two book/movie character wizards seated at our table, Dumbledore from *Harry Potter* and Gandalf from *Lord of the Rings*. They were both dressed in their white and gray wizardry finest with their long white flowing hair and beards. They were quietly talking and writing. Being the highest quality of wizards, they sensed my presence and slowly looked up from their work and right at me!

I wasn't afraid, as I could see by glimmers in their eyes that they were quite pleased about something. It was then that Gandalf slowly held up a small piece of paper, about the size of a 3" × 5" note card. I could see the writing on it, but I was not close enough to make it out. I realized that he wanted me to read it, so I eased my way into the room until I could read what they had written:

> *Strategic Directive*
> *Training Intervention*
> *Transferring Learning to Behavior*
> *Measures and Outcomes*
> *Key Learnings*

I woke up shortly after that and fortunately had enough memory to write it down. The format for the Best Practices Case Studies was basically set.

I have learned so much over the years from my colleagues, even more than from dreams. Most seem to be willing and even eager to share what works for them and what doesn't. I can think of many examples where I have modified my approach to a particular business issue based on advice from others. We hope you find some gems in the following accounts of successful forays into the four levels. We are extremely grateful for each professional's willingness to share what works for them.

FROM DON:

In 1993 when I wrote the book *Evaluating Training Programs: The Four Levels*, I dedicated Part 2 to case studies from organizations that were applying one or more of my levels. The purpose was to provide forms, procedures, designs, and strategies that could be applied or adapted to other organizations. This is one of the reasons the book has been so popular and helpful. So when Jim and I decided to write this book, we knew that case studies would be a valuable part. After selecting a variety of excellent organizations, each was given the following directions:

1. Select a significant and successful training program based on a strategic directive.
2. Focus on best practices, particularly in the area of transferring learning to behavior.
3. Use the common format provided by Jim.

This book has two purposes:

1. To review the four levels for evaluating training programs and relate them to the challenge of transferring learning to behavior.
2. To provide concepts, principles, and techniques for implementing the transfer through Jim's ideas and experiences and through case studies from organizations that have done it!

So, read the case studies and look for ideas you can use and/or adapt to your organization. Although they are built on the same five headings, we allow for some differences in style that reflect different corporate cultures and styles.

Chapter 9

Manufacturing Organizations

Toyota Quality Financial Management

STRATEGIC CHALLENGE

Customer satisfaction indexes in the mid 1990s clearly showed a very high dissatisfaction with the process of financial transactions when buying a vehicle at Toyota dealerships. Customers cited three main reasons for the dissatisfaction:

- Process took too long (sometimes as long as two to four hours)
- Financial services personnel were not honest with information
- Discrepancy with information given by salesperson versus financial services personnel

Toyota Financial Services (TFS) felt that they could discover a way to increase customer satisfaction, but knew they needed to approach the solution from a performance improvement perspective, rather than training solution perspective.

Preliminary Background and Research

The TFS conducted three main activities:

- A group of four associates spent eighteen months researching top-performing dealerships. In some cases they spent a full day observing and interviewing all job functions in Toyota sales departments. They observed and interviewed Dealer Principals, General Managers, Financial Services Managers, and Sales Consultants.
  Important Note: All dealerships are franchises, which means that managers can choose whether or not participate in any improvement program.
- Researchers mystery-shopped public auto retailers that were just coming onto the market and advertised a new of way of doing business.
- A major American captive automobile financing corporation allowed the researchers to visit their training facility for three days. During that time, they were allowed to speak to the facilitators and directors of training. They also observed actual training sessions, which were conducted in a unique learning environment. The environment consisted of large conference rooms with technical capability and arranged in a U shape. They also had smaller, office-sized rooms in which practice sessions could take place and be videotaped for immediate viewing and feedback.

After completing these activities, TFS contracted with Sandy Corporation in 1997 and designed an improvement plan.

TRAINING INTERVENTION

In its design, the full intervention would contain ten important steps. For all ten steps to be completed, TFS recognized a need for more support in branch offices throughout the country to assist the dealers. The position of Performance Development Manager (PDM) was established.

Each PDM would be solely responsible for carrying out the responsibilities of the steps of Toyota Quality Financial Management (TQFM).

Even though the PDMs assisted in Steps 1 through 3 in a minimal way, they would be fully responsible for the dealer's completion of Steps 5 through 10. It is during Steps 5 through 10 that the TQFM participant moves from Level 2 evaluations to Levels 3 and 4. These steps will, therefore, be outlined under Transferring Learning to Behavior.

Following are the first four steps in this process.

Step 1: Dealer orientation meeting

A staff of PDMs will be dedicated to dealership financial services. In this meeting, they will meet with dealership senior management to discuss the process and its benefits to the dealership. A virtual snapshot of a given dealership's financial services performance will be used as a benchmark.

Step 2: Self-assessment

Since product knowledge is a key to customer satisfaction, the professional development continuum begins with an assessment of each participant's current knowledge of relevant fields to diagnose areas for improvement. A 90 percent score allows participants to test out of individual modules.

Step 3: Self-study modules

To provide an adequate level of skills and product-based training, a series of self-study modules was developed to help Financial Services Managers prepare themselves to get the most out of the five-day class. Each module contains product knowledge and describes the features, benefits, and any compliance issues related to each product.

Step 4: University

The University of Toyota conducts a five-day class using state-of-the-art learning technologies, including audience response systems (ARS), videotaped role-playing exercises, teambuilding activities, and one-on-one instruction. All courses are cofacilitated by a dedicated staff, with no more than eighteen participants in any given class.

Russ Mundi, the Retail Education Manager at the School of Retail Professional Development, notes that great effort was made not only to develop an exceptional training process, but to create the right kind of learning environment. The training facility was designed to be a non-threatening place to learn and to practice, with the hope that the inevitable learning curve, and subsequent drop in productivity, would occur *in the training facility and not on the job.*

TRANSFERRING LEARNING TO BEHAVIOR

Russ points out that out of ten steps, *six* actually occur after the formal training is completed. These are the steps that ensure that participants are capable and motivated to apply what they have learned to their actual work.

Step 5: Installation

After a Financial Services Manager graduates from the five-day class, the Performance Development Manager will support the installation of the Customer Satisfaction Process in the dealership. By conducting meetings with the Dealer Principle, General Manager, General Sales Manager, Financial Service Managers, Sales Managers, and the sales staff, the Performance Development Manager will explain how the Customer Satisfaction Process works and the type of teamwork that will be necessary to sustain it.

Step 6: Evaluation

The true test of any development program lies in results, and that's why Toyota Quality Financial Management was designed with integrated measurement tools. To generate some of these measurements, the Performance Development Manager observes the process, offers subsequent feedback and coaching, and helps develop an action plan. A Dealer Performance Report is also utilized as a measurement device to provide feedback for return on investment.

Step 7: Certification

Just as the five-day class supports following up with the customer after the sale, Toyota Quality Financial Management supports following up with Financial Services Managers throughout the continuum, culminating in the Certification Seminar.

Step 8: Advanced seminars

Since professional development must occur on a continuous basis, Toyota Quality Financial Management has been designed to deliver continuous support, which includes a series of advanced seminars.

Step 9: In-dealership consulting

To provide ongoing support, assessment, and process improvement, in-dealership consulting is made available to each participating dealership. A professional performance coach will help the dealership management team define specific consulting needs and customize an improvement strategy.

Step 10: Performance groups

Dealerships that maintain certification are also eligible to participate in a Performance Group. These groups are comprised of Financial Services Managers, Dealer Principles, or General Managers. They meet for one day three times a year to discuss their individual financial services performance as compared to others in the group.

MEASURES AND OUTCOMES

Measurement of the outcomes was done in two ways:

- Dealer Performance Reports (see Step 6 above)
- Evaluations by PDMs following the completion of each step

Measures of productivity, profitability, customer satisfaction, and employee retention were the critical components in the Dealer Performance Reports. These reports were first conducted six months before the intervention began, and they continued for twelve months after the installation of Step 5. The FSM also monitored the Customer Satisfaction Index reports on a monthly basis during that time.

The PDMs were responsible for conducting Steps 5 through 10 and ensuring that the reports of all progress were completed.

The customer satisfaction levels usually increase almost immediately after the first five steps are completed. Other measurements include sales productivity and profitability, which increase steadily as the remainders of the steps are completed.

The number of dealer personnel that have completed the program is very high and their satisfaction with the program continues to encourage dealer participation. The program has gone through some minor changes in the last six years, but remains similar to its first design.

Author's Comments

According to one of this initiative's leaders, Russ Mundi, another significant outcome of the success of this program is sharing these best practices. The original training facility is in California, but an additional facility was recently built in Houston, and another is being constructed in Baltimore. These additional facilities will improve access for managers working in the East and Midwest. Additionally, executives from Japan (the experts in the field of process improvement!) have observed, learned, and replicated the model in Japan. Toyota also not only allows their competitors to visit their production plants, but actually *tutors* them in the process outlined in this case study.

During a recent phone conversation, I had to ask Russ two last questions:

- "Why do suppose so many organizations struggle with this transfer of learning to behavior?" He replied, "Because the steps to cause that to happen are very tedious. Companies often lack the discipline to see them through."

- "All this sharing of your methods and your secrets—what's in it for you?" He said, "That's a good question. The foundation of Toyota's culture is that of partnerships and helping society. For instance, we are deeply concerned about the environment. We also belief in cooperative ventures that benefit the whole industry. And bad press about *any* automaker is bad press for all of us."

Nextel Communications, Inc.

LINKING EVALUATION DATA TO BUSINESS RESULTS AT NEXTEL COMMUNICATIONS

Case Study Coauthored by

Michael D. Barber
Senior Manager, Evaluation
*   & Metrics*
Nextel Communications
Reston, Virginia USA
703-264-4158

Daniel L. Brown
Manager, Evaluation & Metrics
Nextel Communications
Reston, Virginia USA
703-264-4369

STRATEGIC CHALLENGE

The Evolution of HRD

Over the past several years, Nextel's training function has evolved from a decentralized training structure to a centralized Human Resource Development (HRD) department. By centralizing HRD, Nextel has realized efficiencies in the design and development process, gained scalability in deployment efforts, and increased stakeholder satisfaction by linking training to business results. HRD is now viewed as a valued business partner. This case study outlines Nextel's evolution from numerous decentralized training teams into a results-focused HRD department. By telling our story, we hope to share some of our key milestones and best practices related to a focus on results. We will describe the evolution of our evaluation methodology, the use of our online evaluation tool, and the importance of our monthly evaluation round table focus groups.

Reorganization to Human Resource Development

Prior to 2001, training teams were scattered throughout Nextel. Human Resources had a training department that conducted all employee and management training. Customer Service had a training team focused on orientation programs for new customer care representatives. Specialized training teams also existed for sales, IT, and engineering. Some departments had no training support whatsoever. The training professionals in each organization had limited contact with one another to share resources or best practices.

TRAINING INTERVENTION

In 2001, Nextel's Training Council was designed to bring together training professionals from various parts of the company to share resources, ideas, and best practices. The Council was specifically focused on providing Nextel with better business results through training efforts. To determine the effectiveness of training, the Council undertook to develop a robust course evaluation form for use as a company standard. This new form would replace the existing "smile sheet," which simply measured the instructor's effectiveness and how well the course met its stated objectives. The Council desired a better evaluation form to gather data around learning effectiveness, job impact, and business results. This project from the Training Council was the impetus for Nextel's commitment to evaluating business results.

A Results-Focused Vision

As the Training Council began developing the new company-wide evaluation form, plans were in place to centralize the training function into a new department, HRD. Training professionals throughout the company were brought together into one team by which resources could be better utilized across Nextel. The Training Council had already established a need for evaluating training effectiveness, so the commitment to a results-driven team was already in place. During the reorganization, a team within HRD was created to focus on monitoring and tracking training delivery and evaluations metrics. This team was the HRD Performance Center.

When the HRD reorganization took place, many training teams and their training budgets were reallocated to HRD to provide a centralized training function. It was important to educate and communicate to these business owners that the new HRD organization would provide a stronger linkage between each department's training curriculum and Nextel's strategic direction. Specific business unit training managers were created to deliver on this focus, and the Performance Center was created as a support team to the newly implemented training manager role.

The purpose of the Performance Center was to link learning with on-the-job performance. On-the-job performance would be assessed by measuring the increase in knowledge, the improvement in job skills, and tangible business results. The Performance Center began this effort by refining the postcourse evaluation form to gather data related to all levels of evaluation.

TRANSFERRING LEARNING TO BEHAVIOR

Evaluation Roots

As most training organizations use some degree of a Level 1 evaluation for obtaining postcourse data, the dilemma becomes what to do with the paper forms. Nextel was no different in this regard. Our initial Level 1 evaluation captured the typical reactions from the participants and asked if they felt the objectives of the course were met. The Performance Center desired more tangible results linked to job and business impact.

After refining our Level 1 postcourse evaluation, there was still one hurdle to overcome. Although the survey collected data at all learning levels, it was still a paper-based survey. The data collected was valuable, but there was neither enough time nor a cost-effective way to process and analyze the data. At this point the Performance Center knew that another system for capturing training data must be implemented.

An Expanded Focus

An online evaluation system was implemented to gather data at all learning levels and to effectively capture and communicate the findings in a timely manner. From research collected by the KnowledgeAdvisors' Learning Analytics Study, "reasonable quantitative and qualitative indicators are perceived as useful information in the decision making process of senior management."* The study also stated, "Given how executives make decisions, often times reasonable data provided in a more timely manner outweighs data with more precision delivered in a less timely manner."

Working from a similar train of thought, we made the decision to use broad survey questions to gather data at all learning levels. We implemented an online evaluation system to gather our data electronically. To make use of the data, we began with participants postcourse predictions and estimations, and compared them with tangible followup results collected sixty days later from the same participants. It is after analysis and collaboration that we are able to make conscious business decisions. In certain circumstances, Nextel invests the time and resources to conduct highly statistical impact studies. The ability to have the evaluation data collected electronically has greatly decreased the time, cost, and effort required to collect, analyze, and deliver results to our key stakeholders. Having this data readily available has made the Performance Center a strategic partner with all line-of-business leaders when aligning training to business results.

---

*Jeffrey Berk, *Learning Analytics Best Practices Research Study* (Chicago, IL: KnowledgeAdvisors, Inc., 2004).

Evaluation Metrics for Stakeholders

As a strategically driven company, Nextel management expects tangible results from our training efforts. Through our online evaluation system, HRD can provide quantifiable metrics from participant estimations that link learning to performance. Many executives have the evaluation metrics related to business impact, and job impact linked to their monthly balanced scorecard. Business owners use the scorecard to help manage the performance of their team. In this way, HRD can show a direct relationship between training initiatives and business results.

HRD also uses the online evaluation database to flag courses that are not hitting benchmarked targets. For example, all courses require a job impact score of 80 percent or higher. If a course slips below this benchmark, the Performance Center will analyze the results to determine what followup action is necessary. In some cases, the online evaluation data can help determine the cause of the inefficiencies. In other cases, a comprehensive followup survey or focus group is required with past participants to determine why the course is not hitting the mark. With real-time evaluation data available, HRD can quickly react to an ineffective course and make immediate changes. This flexibility and speed help contribute to Nextel's competitive advantage.

Evaluation Metrics as Internal Performance Indicators

Evaluation metrics are used within the HRD department as monthly performance indicators for instructors, instructional designers, and distance learning developers. Instructors are responsible for the satisfaction with the classroom experience, including their teaching style, enthusiasm, responsiveness to students' needs, and the learning environment. Instructor scores are monitored and compared with an internal standard on HRD's monthly scorecard. The performance of instructional designers is also reported on the monthly scorecard by reporting satisfaction scores for course content. Likewise, the satisfaction of the online delivery methods and online courseware is reported as a metric for the distance learning developers. These metrics correlate to a Level 1, reaction/satisfaction, rating in Kirkpatrick's model. Metrics for learning effectiveness, job impact, and business impact are also reported on the monthly scorecard. Responsibility for these metrics is shared between instructors, designers, and the internal customer's primary point of contact. Training evaluation results are consistently discussed at monthly evaluation round table focus groups.

The Evaluation Round Table as a Best Practice

The evaluation round table is a collaborative discussion with the instructors, courseware designers, internal training points of contact, and the Performance Center about a course that may not be meeting the standardized metrics on the HRD scorecard. The Performance Center plays a facilitative role in the discussion. We provide the data collected from the postevent and followup surveys to facilitate an open dialogue.

The structure of the round table includes the following key components:

- Review evaluation learning levels—Review the Kirkpatrick learning levels for a common understanding and vernacular for discussion.

- Map course objectives to learning levels—Review the course objectives and map to the corresponding learning level.

- Review evaluation forms—Review the standard evaluation forms, postevent and followup.

- Report review—Discuss the data collected in the comprehensive reports.

- Small-group brainstorming—Assess what appears to be working and where opportunities for improvement may lie.

The goals of the round table are communicated to the participants of the focus group to establish a clear end in mind. For example, we are able to assess Level 1, participant satisfaction, and Level 2, learning effectiveness, from the training class and use the participant estimations for job impact and business results. Also, we discuss and suggest modifications to content to provide better linkage to job application and learning-to-behavior changes based on the data presented. If learning is taking place from postevent scores but not being transferred to on-the-job performance, we can put a plan in place to determine what possible barriers to implementation exist. The round table benefits include increased communication within HRD and among business owners, offer an avenue for the online evaluations to be used, and provide the basis for linking training to business results.

OUTCOMES

A Commitment to Results

Over the past several years many changes have occurred in Human Resources at Nextel: the formation of a centralized HRD function has been one of the most visible. The support of the vice president of HRD, funding from the organization, and efforts of the Performance Center team have enabled the vision of a results-focused training organization to become a reality.

Implementing the online evaluation system has enabled the entire training organization to capitalize on the availability of training data for continuous improvement, accountability, and linkage to business results. We continue to monitor and report the four key performance indicators on the monthly balanced scorecard for participant satisfaction, learning effectiveness, job impact, and business results to provide a stronger linkage between each department's training curriculum and Nextel's strategic direction. Based on these key performance indicators, we are able to provide the stakeholders of Nextel's training programs the data to engage them through our evaluation round tables. Our effort to provide credible data in a timely manner has begun to prove itself as a cornerstone of the organization and has solidified our position as a strategic business partner.

Hewlett Packard

*TRADITIONAL TRAINING DELIVERY MEETS LIVE
INTERACTIVE WEB-BASED DELIVERY AT
HEWLETT PACKARD*

Developed by Richard Ward

STRATEGIC DIRECTIVE

HP Services sells knowledge and skill packaged as definitive services and capability. These services are designed to provide specific solutions to HP customers. These solutions are usually comprised of HP products and Enterprise-level software applications designed and developed by HP. By definition HP is a total solution provider.

Continuous progress in information technology creates demand for new services as technology enhancements allow concerns, of all types, to solve existing problems and seize new opportunities not before possible. The application of the advances in IT to solve concrete business problems fuels a demand for new IT services. Consequently, new service offerings require that service providers actively pursue new capability development to realize the revenue opportunities created by the emerging service demand.

In traditional manufacturing concerns, the most successful products are the ones that reach the market first. A similar corollary can be drawn for IT service organizations. The speed and uniformity at which new capability development occurs dictates how rapidly a service concern can capture a share of the emerging market for service opportunities and differentiate itself from its competition.

The challenge for IT professional service concerns, HP Services included, is to ensure that capability development occurs *effectively* and *efficiently* in concert with the emerging needs in the marketplace and is maintained at the appropriate level over the life of the technology itself. *Effectively* is intended to mean neither a surplus nor shortage of service delivery resources ever exist to meet emerging demand and achieve organizational revenue goals. *Efficiently* means that the total cost for capability development is such that a financial return can be attributed to the capability development before the need to re-skill service delivery resources.

The speed with which IT technology changes and the amount of change have created considerable challenge for HP Services to effectively and efficiently develop organizational capability. Traditional means of capability development and training (instructor-led training and computer-based training) have become obsolete as a means of delivery given the dynamic nature of IT technology.

To achieve and maintain the highest levels of appropriate, relevant skills and knowledge, HP Services must employ a consistent, holistic worldwide (WW) (the majority of HP's customers are global firms that require the same level of service in all parts of the globe) approach to capability development and training, which minimizes time to capability and the total cost of capability development itself.

The strategic directive was to create and validate "solution (application) development capability" for approximately 1000 (billable) individuals, WW, in order to capture the emerging market for services focused around Microsoft.NET Architecture. Validation of the capability on the individual level was to be partially accomplished through the achievement of .NET MCSD certification that is offered as an alternative in the Microsoft Certified Professional program. Certification requires passage of five exams, four that are preselected and one that can be chosen from several options by the certification candidate.

This goal was to be accomplished within following parameters:

- Completion and verification of skills within a 24-month period to achieve the revenue forecast.
- The program budget goal, which was reduced 50 percent from previous comparable efforts.
- "Opportunity Cost" (time away from job for billable service delivery resources), which needed to be reduced by a minimum of 50 percent from previous WW capability development efforts.

Prior to the initiation of this program, most services focused on application integration and enterprise infrastructure. Solution development represented a considerable re-skilling for HP's service delivery resources, because the competency required for application integration differs greatly from that required for solution development.

TRAINING INTERVENTION

Traditional training delivery by virtue of practice and design limits what the training solution is comprised of. Certain assumptions are usually made regarding an individual's knowledge before attending the training. Additionally, the model assumes the instructor will provide what is required by the learner to ensure the experience is a productive one. Consequently the training materials usually consist of standard curricula that support a lecture format and standard laboratory exercises to reinforce it. In addition it is assumed that the learner leaves the class having acquired and being able to apply new knowledge. Conversely traditional computer-based training provides only the most basic instruction with little feedback to the learners.

Armed with the knowledge that experience has provided (two prior WW efforts to train and certify a combined total of 3000 Microsoft MCSEs), considerable effort was expended to define the components that would be required to ensure success.

Considering lessons learned in conjunction with the business parameters of the program, a live online training solution was defined. To eliminate the weakness usually associated with online training, this solution included an instructor within an interactive virtual classroom.

To address the size of the audience and diversity of learning styles, the learning solution was crafted from multiple components designed to alert the learner to their specific knowledge deficiencies and provide the means to address those deficiencies.

Learning sessions were held for two hours each day, three days each week for ten weeks to address the material in the twenty-five days (approximately 200 hours of class and 140 of billable time) of lecture lab training that was available from Microsoft for the same topics. It should be noted that the online format eliminated duplicative content and reduced total training time by 50 percent.

The learning solution contained the following components:

1. *.Net Advisor CD.*

2. *Precourse knowledge assessments*—To enable the student to focus on knowledge deficiencies.

3. *Postcourse knowledge assessment*—To identify and reinforce areas the students know well or areas where additional focus might be required.

4. *Microsoft official curriculum*—To ensure consistency WW, minimize solution cost, and ensure the solution was current and available when required.

5. *Online interactive lab exercises*—To reinforce lecture content and help ensure that students progressed through the learning curve rapidly.

6. *Mentoring*—To provide clarity when and if required.

7. *Online technical publications*—To provide reinforcement of training materials, support interactive labs, ensure material was readily available, and minimize logistical considerations.

8. *Practice exams for certification*—To familiarize first-time certification seekers with the format and flow of a certification exam.

9. *Unlimited session playback capabilities*—To allow for those who required additional reenforcement or for those whose job responsibilities called them away from individual daily sessions during the training.

Internet Meets Tradition . . . Head On

While maintaining the value the instructor brings to learners experience, this solution eliminated the cost of travel and lodging and minimized the most costly aspect of any training intervention, opportunity costs, by scheduling sessions to minimize time away from the job.

TRANSFERRING LEARNING TO BEHAVIOR

This was accomplished in five key ways.

Coaching

Coaching was applied in two areas. Before individuals were selected for the program, a set of preliminary screening criteria was established for use by the program drivers in each region. One of the responsibilities of the program drivers was to consult with business management to identify individuals who should be enrolled in the program. Advice was provided to business management, through the program drivers, that individuals selected for the program should meet or exceed the screening criteria to maximize the probability of success in the program.

The second form of coaching was directed at the certification candidates themselves. In addition to leading the delivery of content, the instructors were available via telephone or dedicated chat rooms to provide feedback and give direction based upon assessment results, answer specific questions, and provide clarification on complex topics.

Observation

The sheer size of the audience rendered one-to-one observation impossible. However, the sophistication of HP's CERTrak (certification tracking database) allowed us to produce a monthly snapshot of the progress toward certification. It should be noted that monthly electronic updates were provided on each individual enrolled in the program by Microsoft.

Enrollment and training dates were used as baselines to completion of the first exam. The dates of the first exam and each exam thereafter were used to determine average time between exams. Those individuals who fell outside the norm were contacted to determine if they required additional assistance to complete the required exams.

Feedback

Two feedback methods were employed. Level 1 evaluations were employed to ensure that the total learning solution was meeting the needs of the audience. In addition, the revenue performance of the program and customer satisfaction information were employed as secondary indicators that the capability had been developed and could be applied to solve customer problems.

Knowledge Transfer

One of the aims of the program was to certify the individuals who had taken online training. To help ensure that these individuals had the knowledge to pass the certification exams, live online exam preparation sessions were created. Certification is not the final measure of knowledge transfer, but it is a reasonable indicator. To date over 75 percent of trainees have become certified as application developers.

Financial Leverage

To attend the training students utilized their own PCs from their own locations to attend the class, and all lab exercises are facilitated through the use of remote online interactive sessions delivered within the context of the training itself. Sessions are scheduled in two-hour blocks three days each week, using a single hour per day of billable time.

OUTCOMES

The following summary data includes assumptions regarding

- Average hourly billable rate (example) and utilization (opportunity costs)
- Average travel costs
- Average lodging costs
- Average meal costs
- Tuition costs
- Average class size
- Average number of students per class

Table 3. Total Cost Projections

	Year 1	Year 2	Grand Total
Traditional delivery			
Total organizational costs	6465300	6681465	13146765
Total cost per student	12677.059	13100.91176	12888.985
Cost per full student day	507.08235	524.0364706	515.55941
Online live delivery			
Total organizational costs	1892100	1981350	3873450
Total cost per student	3710	3885	3797.5
Cost per full student day equivalent	371	388.5	397.75

Table 4. Cost Comparison

	Traditional delivery	Live online delivery	Delta favoring live online delivery
Cost comparison			
Total organization costs	13146765	3873450	−9273315
Cost per student	12888.99	3797.5	−9091.49
Payback analysis			
Total cost per individual	12888.99	3797.5	−9091.49
Increased weekly revenue	700	700	0.00
Payback in weeks	18.41	5.43	−12.99

- Number of classes per year
- Inflation over a two-year period

The online learning solution saved over $9000 per student over traditional training delivery. The training resulted in an average 5 percent increase in billable time per week. Given the reduced cost and the increase in billable hours, the organization realized a payback on the training investment in less than 5.5 weeks.

Reduction in Turnover

If history is an indication, approximately 100—or 10 percent—of those engaged in the training program would have voluntarily left HP. As a result of the training program, approximately sixty individuals who were in the program voluntarily left the company.

	With program	Without program	Delta
Voluntary departure from HP	60	100	40
Total cost to locate and hire*	$2,400,000	$4,000,000	$1,600,000

*Assumes search costs and 30 days of unproductive time at the outset of employment

Effective and Efficient Time to Capability

Time to capability translates into increased revenue and profit for HP Services. Statistics indicate that time to capability averages sixteen elapsed weeks after a program participant is identified. Note also that the total time is considered acceptable given that services demand was accelerating at the same time capability development was occurring, thereby ensuring little surplus or shortage in service delivery resources. All revenue targets for the program have been exceeded.

RESULTS AND LESSONS LEARNED

- The training strategy was correct!
  - 1000+ individuals trained WW in 16 months
    - 100 percent of individuals trained in 66 percent of elapsed program duration
    - Student response overwhelmingly positive, as communicated through evaluations
    - A total cost reduction of $10.8M, exceeding program goals
- Select a full-service training provider to enable greater flexibility in component-based solutions and meet a wider audience need

- Slight initial cost increase offset by accelerated capability development

- Continually evaluate solution components

- Ensures maximum effectiveness and payback of the solution

Ingersoll-Rand, Von Duprin Division

*Submitted by: Minh Trinh and
Dean Lacopetti*

STRATEGIC CHALLENGE

Executives at Von Duprin, a division of Ingersoll-Rand, recently decided that they would initiate Pathway To Excellence (PTE) that drives World Class Performance. PTE is a disciplined process of change that focuses an organization on its strategic directions as the organization develops competitive advantages to achieve World Class Performance. Through this process, PTE aligns programs of change behaviors, metrics, and goals to achieve these strategic directions in three years. With its four phases of developing competencies—Area of Development, Mechanical Compliance, Understanding and Utilization, and Perpetuation—PTE emphasizes accountability, ownership, and continual measurement, which provide a structure for sustainable and transferable change. The use of metrics and scorecards help to identify and align global strategies with individual performances, as well as to monitor for continuous improvement and achievements that can be celebrated. In short, the PTE process helps to dramatically transform businesses to a competitive World Class Performance operation. For IR–Von Duprin, the ultimate purpose of this strategic challenge is to command the position of market leader in a globally competitive environment.

The specific challenge outlined here is to see how an individual, Minh Trinh, trains, coaches, and leads her industrial associates to successfully implement rapid changes using the PTE process. Minh, a process engineer who works in the Indianapolis division, used the PTE process concepts of "working with strength" and the training methodology of "teaching, showing, coaching, monitoring, and signing off." Minh followed the PTE process as she led change and as she trained her industrial associates to lead their specific changes for improvement. The following is Minh's account of how the process unfolded.

TRAINING INTERVENTION AND TRANSFERRING LEARNING TO BEHAVIOR

We took many steps to implement this new PTE process throughout the plant. First, leaders of our division continue to extensively train and educate all of their employees to ensure that we understand the philosophies, concepts, metrics, and processes to the PTE. The leadership team left many of the specific methods on how and when to apply the principles to those who would do the actual work. We decided to start practicing these principles and concepts in our first initiative—to improve the processes in the Trim department in order to create a more World Class Performance environment.

The goal was to change the Trim assembly process from batch manufacturing to a flow process, which efficiently flows the product while optimizing the capacity of equipment, floor space, and operators' time. We met with the production team and explained what we were planning to do, why we have chosen this course of action, and that we would need all of their help and support through this dramatic quick change. I knew that my biggest challenge was to get the employees—many whom have been with Von Duprin for many years—to participate or lead any of the changes to come.

Through a period of four months, the Trim department quickly transformed its assembly process from ten individually operated assembly cells to three mix-model flow lines. Throughout the change process, employees actively participated in the design, testing, and implementation of the new processes.

As a result of the quick changes, the material and equipment within the production areas became very disorganized. There was a definite need to improve the workplace organization (WPO). I decided to apply PTE's process of "working with strength" and train the associates to lead this final project.

Listed are the steps that occurred as associates were trained to understand and utilize the tools needed to improve WPO through a process called 5S—Sort, Set in order, Shine, Standardize, and Sustain. It also explains the steps that were taken in teaching, showing, coaching, and monitoring the associates to ensure they applied or used the tools they learned.

1. Through the use of PTE issue boards, a tool structured to empower employees to identify and resolve issues, associates communicated the issue that disorganization of material and equipment in the department was a problem affecting production. To resolve this issue board item, I set up teams of associates who would volunteer to work on resolving this issue. As a team, we decided to declare a WPO WAR on each of the different production areas. "WAR" is an acronym for With All Resources—meaning it is a concentrated, extraordinary effort of focus, with intensity and 100 percent involvement of all people to solve the task at hand.

2. On the first day of the WPO WAR, I set the agenda, communicated expectations to the team members, trained the team on 5S processes, and taught them the tools they would use such as creating and managing a formal action list. By benchmarking other areas within the plant, I showed the team applications of 5S and ideas for improvement. In setting expectations, I clarified to the team that I would not be leading them, but rather would act more as a coach or mentor in guiding them through this WPO WAR. I then explained the team leader's responsibilities, which included presenting the team's process and results to management and their coworkers, and asked for a volunteer.

3. After the training, the associates assessed the production line area that they would be improving. From this initial assessment, they determine and record their own goals for improvement. Determining and recording their goals gave them a clear understanding of their expected results. As a coach, I praised them on their good thoughts and only intervened when I felt they had missed an opportunity or were getting off track.

4. After team goals were set, the associates created an action list using the formal spreadsheet documents I had provided. The initial step in creating this action list was to record the problems they saw within the area. As I monitored their progress, I noticed the associates were using examples of problems they had seen from the 5S training and benchmarks in identifying problems within the area. As a result, the associates generated a list of forty-six problems. In conjunction with creating a list, the associates took digital pictures of the problems they were seeing within the area to capture the "before" state. Unexpectedly, the associates themselves decided to make further use of the pictures by printing and posting all forty-six pictures in the department to communicate to their coworkers why it was important for this team

to improve the area and how the coworkers themselves contribute to the problems.

5. After the action list was generated, the associates determined a solution and prioritized the list. The lead associate then took ownership of the action list, managing it for completion and status of items on the list. This worked very well because the associates were not only directing the team on tasks to be completed, but also taking responsibility for directing maintenance personnel on jobs to be completed.

6. As a coach, I continued to support the team by:

   a. Removing barriers such as time limitations and other unassociated responsibilities the industrial associates normally had.

   b. Uncovering and resolving concerns among the team members. For example, sometimes the associates were unsure about a change they wanted to make because they were concerned that their coworkers or supervisor would not like the change. I resolved such concerns by initiating communication among the groups.

   c. Making sure resources were readily available. For example, I always made sure the team had the proper equipment, tools, maintenance support, and additional labor when needed.

   d. Actively assisting with all necessary changes showing the associates I supported their decisions and was ready to work hard to make it happen.

   e. Endeavoring to make the event more enjoyable by doing special things like bringing in special lunches.

7. After the five-day WPO WAR event, the industrial associates continued to self-manage their action list, improving and sustaining the organizational changes by using PTE's 5-Star audit process (a 50-step daily audit of desired behaviors). At the end, we celebrated by taking them out to lunch.

OUTCOMES

Outcomes can be both objective and subjective. Here are some of the objective results after all improvements in the Trim department were made:

- Required production floor space reduced by 1120 sq.ft. (4355 to 3235 sq.ft.)

- Production rate increase by 50 per shift (800 to 850)
- Department staffing decreased by one (21 to 20)

. . .

Minh and the team made impressive progress. To assess and evaluate subjective results, I (Jim) spent some time at Von Duprin with them. I asked them questions to see what benefits they see from this change initiative. Here is what I heard:

Minh: Pathway To Excellence's concept of "working with strength" really gave me the idea and basis to empower the employees. This was a great learning experience for me as it allowed me to see that given the right amount of training, coaching, support, and accountability, the industrial associates accomplished more than any of us thought possible. Plus, it took a lot of the stress off of me. I was especially pleased when associates such as Amanda and Audrey—who have worked here for over twenty-five years and rarely participated in such change activities—were significant contributors to the team throughout the change process.

Martha: I am a group leader here. I helped to design methods of getting the materials closer to the workers and reorganized workstations and areas so that the work flowed more smoothly. I feel less stress at work now, and know that many other people do, too. I am proud of what we did, and know I can do this elsewhere in the plant if asked to.

Liza: We started this whole thing to improve the flow of our product. When problems were uncovered, the group decided how to make changes. Look here at these plastic signs hung over the material for identification [smiling]. It was my idea to do this, and now it has gone through the entire plant. This was all about putting ideas into practice, and to work as a team instead of individually. [I asked Liza what role Minh played in the success of this venture.] She bought lunch for us! [laughing] She asked for and listened to our input into problems and solutions, shared her good ideas, and gave us the resources we needed.

KEYS TO SUCCESS

- Start with a strong, logical strategy to close gaps and achieve world-class performance.
- Explain the rationale of why we are changing.

- Teach this logical strategy to all employees.
- Treat everyone with respect, and allow him or her to get involved to whatever level possible.
- Communicate expectations.
- Teach, show, coach, and monitor!
- Show support and provide resources.
- Give responsibilities and accountability. Allow them to lead—empower them.
- Follow up with coaching and additional training. Test for understanding, and measure and reinforce new behavior as well as results.

Chapter 10

Service Organizations

Nicco Internet Ventures Limited

MOVING UP THE LEVELS: APPLYING THE FOUR-LEVEL
FRAMEWORK OF TRAINING EVALUATION

Submitted by: Sugato Lahiry, Vice President, HR Services

Nicco Internet Ventures Ltd. (NILV), set up by the Nicco Group, a diversified Indian conglomerate, is a premier IT-enabled HR solutions and services company. NIVL provides comprehensive and cost-effective recruitment solutions to its clients, using the latest technologies and processes. The offerings include:

- Search and selection services
- Headhunting and boutique assignments

- Turn-key recruitment assignments
- Customized recruitment solutions to suit clients' specific needs

Apart from providing end-to-end recruitment solutions to organisations, NIVL has core expertise and offers a broad range of HR services and solutions in areas such as competency-based people management applications, rewards management and compensation surveys, performance management systems, and employee surveys.

NIVL's Campus Solutions range of services includes services and solutions covering to the gamut of placement, employability skills assessment, and workplace readiness training activities for academic and professional institutions.

The IT solutions wing of NIVL offers workable, robust, and technically superior IT solutions and consulting services using a variety of technologies and platforms. The range of services and solutions includes:

- Internet and intranet solutions
- E-commerce and m-commerce
- Corporate communication and multimedia services
- Software solutions

STRATEGIC CHALLENGE

The consultants for the search and selection (S&S) line of business were hired from other small, medium, and large search and selection firms over the three years that NIVL has been operating. Though nearly all of them had formal management education with specialization in Human Resources, they had little or no experience in negotiating with clients.

The job profile of the S&S consultants at NIVL was designed to attract and retain the right talent by providing enriched job content. The job of an S&S consultant included business development, search and selection, and client relationship management. The task category of business development in turn included negotiating with prospective clients on rate of professional charges for the services rendered.

The S&S industry comprises small and medium players, primarily proprietorship firms, that work within a narrow band of professional charges, usually ranging from 8.33 to 12.5 percent of the annual compensation of the candidates the firms helped their clients hire.

The S&S consultants at NIVL who were responsible for discussing, negotiating, and reaching an agreement with new clients on the rate of professional charges often tended to fall in a rut during the negotiation stage. They tended to go about the process of negotiation with clients in a stereotyped manner, beginning by presenting standard NIVL professional charge rates to the clients. Their actions generally reflected an urge to conclude the negotiation process as quickly as possible, suggesting an apathy toward the process and resorting to one of the following behaviours:

- As soon as the client asked for lowering of the rates they would refer the case to their managers and seek specific instructions.
- They would agree to lower the rate to 8.33 percent, often without exploring intermediate rates such as 10 percent.
- They would close the negotiation by refusing to move from the standard rate, displaying a sort of "take it or leave it" stance. (This was the least frequent response.)

Negotiating difficulty proved to be a rather serious performance issue in a tough and competitive market, in which margins seemed to be in a perpetual state of free-fall, largely because of heavy price cuts resorted to by smaller firms.

An analysis of the problem, carried out by in-depth interviews of consultants, brought out the following issues:

- Inadequate understanding of the negotiation process
- Inadequate knowledge and skill required for negotiating effectively
- A diffident attitude: "Negotiating is tough business and I won't be able to handle it."

This analysis clearly indicated a knowledge-skill-attitude issue that could be effectively remedied through training.

TRAINING INTERVENTION

A training course was developed for helping the S&S consultants develop the following exit competencies:

- Appreciate the importance of planning and preparation in successful negotiation.
- Identify a set of negotiating objectives and outcomes ranging from the "ideal" to "acceptable."

- Plan, prepare, and execute a strategy for emerging from the negotiation process with major gains and minor losses.

The training course employed lecturettes, exercises, games, and skill practice sessions to cover the following topics:

- Why effective business negotiations are win-win negotiations
- The principles of win-win negotiation
- How to prepare for negotiation through

  - Collecting information on the other party
  - Framing negotiating objectives and outcomes
  - Identifying multiple negotiating variables (items that can be negotiated on)
  - Costing all the negotiating variables
  - Identifying possible trade-off points
  - Identifying cost of concessions vis-à-vis the value gain in a trade-off

- How to set up a negotiating agenda
- How to move through the agenda smoothly
- How to overcome roadblocks, if any
- How to close a negotiation

All the S&S consultants underwent the training course.

A summative evaluation of the training course at Level 1 revealed the following reactions:

Table 5.

	Strongly Agree %	Agree %	Undecided %	Disagree %	Strongly Disagree %
Gained important new knowledge	91	9			
Gained important new skills	82	18			
Would help me in negotiating with clients effectively	91	9			

Evaluation at Level 2 done through pre- and posttraining quizzes showed a gain from 24 to 92 percent correct answers.

Even as these intermediate measures were collected for assessing the efficacy of the training course, we realized that all these would be irrelevant if the consultants were not able to achieve better outcomes from the negotiating process. In other words, the training would be considered to have achieved its objectives only if the consultants were able to negotiate better deals from their clients.

The training intervention was designed, developed, and implemented to solve a business problem: falling margins owing to the inability of the consultants to get the clients to agree to rates commensurate with the quality of service provided. This is an essential business skill for the given task situation. The training was not born out of any esoteric or less fundamental reason.

TRANSFERRING LEARNING TO BEHAVIOR

The high stakes of this training were quite obvious. It provided a unity of purpose from both the business managers' perspective and the training perspective. Thus it was decided to employ two basic mechanisms to ensure that the training translated into a sustained and consistent deployment of the newly acquired knowledge, skills, and attitudes (KSAs) in actual work situations.

Reward Reinforcement

The consultants were included in an incentive plan focused on the net billing value of the professional services rendered. The net billing value, in turn, was directly linked with the rate of professional charges negotiated with the client. Thus the amount of incentive a consultant could earn depended on, among other things, the rate of charges. Other things being equal, the higher the rate of charges, the more money a consultant would earn by way of incentive.

This linkage between higher rates of professional charges and the earning potential through incentive was highlighted and emphasized throughout the training course, as well as during weekly review meetings after the training.

Task Reinforcement

The reinforcement process through reward (rate of charge–incentive linkage) was no doubt a very potent motivational force for the consultants to deploy the newly acquired (desired) behaviours. However, it was considered a necessary but not sufficient condition to ensure that the new KSAs would translate consistently into new behaviours.

Hence, it was decided also to employ a simple task-level mechanism to strengthen the KSA–work behaviour sequence. The consultants were required to prepare and present a negotiating plan to their managers before they embarked on negotiation with a client. This process helped ensure that the consultants leveraged their new learning.

Beyond Level 2

The nature of the posttraining work behaviour in question and the context in which it was performed made any kind of direct observation impractical. To what extent the consultants were deploying the newly acquired KSAs in their actual work situation could only be inferred from other pieces of evidence. The other source of information in this case was debriefing sessions held with the consultants by their managers immediately after a negotiating session.

The debriefing interviews with the consultants revealed the following:

- The prenegotiation presentation helped the consultants discover new information about clients.

- Such information combined with other aspects of the preparation gave the consultants a high degree of confidence during the negotiation.

- The consultants got better at negotiation with practice. They felt that their skills improved through successive rounds of negotiating exposure.

- Sometimes the purchasing muscle of the client influenced the negotiating outcome to a large extent, and application of new KSAs did not make much difference. However, the consultants saw such cases in the perspective of power economics and did not feel that such cases made negotiating plans redundant in any way.

- The consultants initially resisted spending time in preparation for negotiation, but in the end they felt that the hard work paid off handsomely.

Table 6.

Rate of professional charges negotiated with clients	Percentage of contracts negotiated before training	Percentage of contracts negotiated after training
12.5% and above	33	44
10%	22	19
8.33% and below	45	37

OUTCOMES

Strong line management involvement in training and posttraining reinforcement made it imperative to look for more tangible evidence that the training was paying off. An analysis of the rates of charges negotiated with clients before and after training revealed interesting trends (Table 6).

The upward shift in rates negotiated with clients after the training provides some measure of Level 4 evaluation. Though negotiation outcomes are influenced by other economic and business variables (such as boom/gloom cycle, purchasing muscle of the client, and the extent of competition), it can be safely argued that these factors have largely remained constant since September 2003, when the training was held, and consequently the improvement in rates is an evidence of training effectiveness.

More importantly, the line management, which does not much care for scientific proof and is more often than not satisfied with suggestive evidence, felt enthused with the improvement in results.

KEY DRIVERS OF SUCCESS

What do we need to ensure that classroom training successfully transfers to the work situation and to ensure that we get tangible results from training investments? Analysis of the present case strongly suggests the following:

- *Strategic perspective.* The training intervention in this case was purely a strategic response—a strategic means to achieve a business end. The strategic linkage with business goals made it easy for all involved parties to commit strongly to training success.

- *Alignment of priorities.* The priorities of the line management and those of training were very well aligned. This unity of purpose helped support the transfer of learning from the classroom to the work situation.

- *Ownership and commitment.* The alignment of priorities resulted in very strong ownership of the line management that helped reinforce application of new KSAs in posttraining situations.

- *Strong line of sight.* The interests of the trainees were also very well aligned with the objective of the training, and the line of sight was strong and clear for them. The consultants clearly saw that successful application of the new skills would lead to increased incentive earning for them. This reinforced the transfer process through generating internal drive in the consultants.

- *Management actions.* Requiring the consultants to prepare and present a negotiation plan prior to actual negotiation, recognizing successful performance (of new behaviour) widely in various forums, and showcasing early success helped reinforce the newly acquired KSAs.

ABN AMRO Bank

CASE STUDY—BUILDING CAPABILITY AT ABN AMRO WHOLESALE CLIENTS SERVICES

Raymond Madden
Head of Learning
ABN AMRO Bank

Robert Dick
Programme Director
Executive Education Europe Ltd.

STRATEGIC CHALLENGE

The learning and development challenge was to build capability in the wholesale banking operations area using business-driven action learning. Action learning as defined by Revans* and further developed by others is not new. However, the focus of this case study is how ABN AMRO is encouraging strategic innovation, value creation, and mar-

---

*Reg Revans, *The ABC of Action Learning* (Krieger Publishing Co., 1983).

ket differentiation through a change management program called Building Capability. Two programs exist: Building Capability I for Vice Presidents (VP) lasting five days and Building Capability II for Senior Vice Presidents (SVP), three days followed by a further two days. What was the strategic rationale for Building Capability I and II?

- ABN AMRO wholesale banking strategic positioning:
  - The strategic imperative for the wholesale bank is to be in the top five with respect to a chosen peer group when measured against total shareholder return (TSR).
  - Our client-led model is underpinned by the ability to innovate in the market place, create value for clients and the bank, and allocate capital effectively.
  - Capitalize on an extensive global network of ABN AMRO staff in almost sixty countries to build leading-edge businesses capability.
- The competitive landscape:
  - In a complex, dynamic, competitive landscape, recognizing your competitors' capabilities and strategic direction is a key enabler.
  - To formalize competitor analysis and to create stretch targets for the organization, a process of peer group benchmarking was introduced.
  - TSR is a common measure for evaluating performance in publicly quoted companies. However, connecting TSR to everyday performance of individuals is a challenge for all organizations that have successfully implemented value-based management (VBM).
- Value-based management (Managing for Value):
  - In 2000, ABN AMRO adopted its own VBM, and the "Managing for Value" [MfV] was introduced. MfV became the way to manage the business systemically. It had three models:
    - Business model—A strategic understanding of the sources and drivers of value
    - Management model—Seek out highest value activities using clear metrics in a formal process that evaluates choices.

- People model—A culture of clear accountability and transparency to drive high individual and business performance.

- MfV identifies the true drivers of profitability at all levels in the organization—it provides full transparency. It deploys a common language, framework, and standards for managerial decision-making and unites management around value creation as the key business activity.

- Supporting the business agenda:

  - Learning and development were intimately involved in executing the MfV project.

  - It was recognized that MfV required significant shifts in behavior at all levels of management. Key to the success of MfV implementation was its adoption by managers at the VP and SVP levels.

  - Two management development programs were introduced to support the transition, Building Capability I and II.

  - Given the applied nature of MfV, it was decided to incorporate a business-driven action learning element into the program. This took the form of a Business Improvement Project and Messages to Management.

TRAINING INTERVENTION

What do the programs look like?

- Themes:

  - BC I—Managing for Value, competition and markets, creating value, strategy implementation
  - BC II—Managing for Value, global business, client orientation, strategic thinking

- Objectives of BC I:

  - Engage VPs, as individuals and a management cadre, in their roles as business drivers and managers of resources.
  - Understand markets and competition and how to create business opportunities.
  - Instill the confidence to have strategic dialogues internally and with clients.

- Increase teamwork and networking across the VP group, to the benefit of the business.
- Embed MfV across the business.

- Objectives of BC II:

  - Engage SVPs, as individuals and a management cadre, in their roles as business drivers and managers of resources. Build the will to lead.
  - Focus on wholesale banking and the global competitive landscape.
  - Overcome organizational barriers to innovation and the creation of new business opportunities.
  - Support a culture of client service as a market differentiator.
  - Build the capability to have strategic dialogues internally and with clients.
  - Increase global teamwork and collaboration across the SVP cohort, to the benefit of the business.
  - Embed MfV across the business.

- Participants:

  - VPs and SVPs in either client-facing or specialist product areas and back office functions
  - Global network fully represented

- Content summary of BC I:

  - Managing for Value at ABN AMRO
  - Creating value for customers—Avoiding the commodity trap
  - Creating value through people management
  - Organizations and change
  - Strategic innovation and value creation
  - Creating value
  - Business Improvement Project

- Content summary of BC II:

  - Managing for Value at ABN AMRO
  - The global investment banking industry—The competitive landscape

- Global customers and value creation
- Client-centered organizations
- Strategic choices in value creation

- Messages to management

- Style:

  - The program is designed to be highly interactive and discursive in format. A significant volume of material is delivered interactively through the workshops and case studies rather than through a didactic approach.

  - Contributors come from leading business schools, consultancies, ABN AMRO Academy, and top management.

- Linking content to projects and messages, and later to new behaviors:

  - All contributors are required to support participants in the elaboration of their projects and messages, for example, highlighting content that may have particular applicability.

  - In all presentations, contributors allow for discussion on projects and messages. What kinds of practical issues should be addressed? How do they fit in the MfV framework? How should recommendations for action be couched to get attention?

  - The program director provides surgeries to permit groups or individuals the opportunity to work through the content and presentation of projects or messages.

TRANSFERRING LEARNING TO BEHAVIOR

What were the support and accountability behaviours and processes to ensure application?

- Business Improvement Projects [BIP]:

  - Participants are required to set up a business project for themselves (or in pairs), which they deliver to their line managers eight weeks after the program.

  - Ideas can come from work-related activities on which the participant is currently working, observations on other parts of wholesale, topics they have discussed with their line manager, or concepts that have been discussed with program contributors.

- Projects must have a value-creating focus and preferably have an external orientation; they must be client linked. Projects should be commercially viable and capable of exploitation by a business unit with immediate, measurable, beneficial effect using existing resources.

- Projects are not intended to examine internal ABN AMRO processes.

- BIPs have specific backing from wholesale top management, and line managers are encouraged to give support to participants.

- Over time, it is hoped to generate mini–ABN AMRO case studies that can be used in future programs.

- Messages to Management [MMs]:

  - MMs take another approach to business-driven action learning. Their use recognizes that senior managers may have substantive ideas that others could implement.

  - MMs are delivered to a top management representative in a face-to-face presentation format. Actionable ideas are taken forward by the executive.

  - The screening criteria are similar to BIPs (see above), but the level of research is necessarily at a macro level.

- Website:

  - A dedicated website captures all BIPs and MMs, and access is given to top management, learning and development as well as the participants themselves. It serves as a record over time of the outputs from Building Capability I and II.

  - The website promotes peer group recognition and acts as a spur to those wishing to create visibility for themselves and their ideas.

- Sponsoring managers:

  - Managers who sponsor participants are intimately involved in the development process; firstly, through conducting a pre-program interview to discuss the participant's objectives for attending the program. These objectives are published and reexamined at the program end.

- After the program, the interview is repeated and an action plan drawn up to encourage transfer of learning to the workplace. The interview coincides with delivery of the BIP, which itself is a powerful stimulus to new thinking and action. Sponsoring managers approve the topic for the BIP and assist the participant in its completion.

OUTCOMES

- Networking around projects and messages
- Examples of BIPs:

  - Focus on Central Europe—Global strategy and how to apply standards
  - Establish insight of global integrated energy bankers' view of client-focused information.
  - Challenge German counterparts using Economic Profit models.
  - Cross-selling treasury products
  - Linking service and products in Greater China
  - Improving the market risk approval process for business in India

- Examples of Messages to Management:

  - Extend Brazilian operating model to other countries and regions.
  - Management empowerment: engaging our people
  - Creating client value through increased collaboration
  - New business and governance model for emerging markets
  - Marketing and Advertising (M&A) in Europe
  - Globalizing MIS

Conclusions

- Business Improvement Projects and Messages to Management in transferring learning to the workplace have been very effective from an organizational perspective. Managers are engaged very early in the process and therefore feel a genuine connection to real business challenges.
- The profile of the program is such that individual members of deal teams have taken part in the programs over a two-year pe-

riod. Many VPs have benefitted from the development associated with presenting their ideas to senior management with
whom they may not interact with frequently.

- A number of the BIPs have resulted in new revenue opportunities that have come about by cross-border collaboration from
  program participants.

- A greater understanding of MfV and the drivers behind how
  value is created and destroyed across our businesses.

- The programs are evaluated to Kirkpatrick Levels 1 and 2 routinely. To date, 100 percent of participants recommend the program to colleagues. Some 25 percent of the VP population is
  evaluated to Level 3 by structured interviews six months after
  program completion. No plans are in place to measure to Level
  4 (ROI), although the business deals that result from participants who meet on the program have to date covered the full
  cost of the program by a significant multiplier.

- Business-driven action learning is highly effective if projects are
  specific and engage both participants and their managers in the
  process.

Anthem Blue Cross and Blue Shield

FRONTLINE LEADERSHIP: TEAM LEAD DEVELOPMENT PROGRAM

Submitted by:

Susanne Elsey
Senior Consultant Leadership
  and Associate Development
Bonnie Arend
HR Consultant

Kellie Fehr
Senior Consultant Leadership
  and Associate Development

STRATEGIC DIRECTIVE

Anthem Blue Cross and Blue Shield strives to be among the best and
biggest in their industry by delivering the best product value with the
best people. The company's focus on their people extends to their

Human Resources mission to "Drive Anthem's success by unleashing the potential of great people." Combine these elements with a strategic directive to "provide distinctive service and become easy to do business with," and you will begin to understand the driving force behind the 2003 Anthem Midwest Frontline Leadership Team Lead Development Program initiative.

One measure of Anthem's effectiveness is based on a corporate-wide associate survey conducted by the Great Places to Work Institute. This annual survey showed results that caused the company to take a serious look at their priorities in 2002. There was a significant difference in the level of satisfaction and loyalty between management and other associates. Specifically, an organizational assessment along with the survey scores for frontline associates indicated a perceived lack of feedback and communication from their managers and their support staff of team leads. Anthem's Midwest Region decided to focus attention on both critical leadership roles. This case study centers on the critical role of team lead for technical support, coaching, and leadership in daily workflow to the frontline associates that provide service directly to Anthem's twelve million members. Effectiveness of this group of associates is imperative to be the preferred health insurance and employee benefits organization.

TRAINING INTERVENTION

Audience—Anthem's Team Leads consisted of a group of nearly 300 associates defined as informal leaders. Although they did not have responsibility for managing associates, they had daily leadership responsibilities including technical coaching, feedback, and workflow direction. The Frontline Leadership Team Lead Development Program included five months of prelaunch assessment and design and a year of delivery. Significant planning went into the program to ensure that each level was evaluated and measured, through results and ROI, to achieve success. The stated objective of the program was to "assess and develop front line leaders to ensure proper role fit, in order to increase associate satisfaction and improve organizational performance."

Program—The following elements were included in the training program:

- Pre- and postcompetency model talent assessment
- Monthly classroom training modules

- 360° feedback and development planning
- On-the-job application assignments
- E-learning
- Development peer support team
- Multilevel feedback and coaching
- Assessment of testing, behavioral role-play, and transference to job
- Accountability elements
- Measures of success
- Recognition and reward

The purpose and business case was communicated to all stakeholders. An orientation session clearly defined the role and expectations for the team lead position. It also defined the roles of program participants, management, and Human Resources throughout the program. The vision and major strategies were reviewed, and the parameters of the program clearly explained. Executives and senior managers participated in this process and throughout the program by sharing the rationale, expected outcomes, and rewards.

Specific business results expected as a result of improved leadership effectiveness included

- BIG changes in attitude and positive can-do behaviors
- Efficiencies and productivity improvements leading to reduced administrative expenses
- Increased membership (customers) and membership retention
- Increased service scores
- Improved quality and service

This development program was carefully designed throughout as a business partnership between Anthem's Human Resources and the various lines of business. The program was sponsored by two executive vice presidents who assisted with the planning and had accountability for success at the executive team level. Managers participated in the orientation as well as a mid-program development and check-in session with the team leads. Executive directors also participated in the orientation and the final development assessments that concluded the program.

Participants were expected to learn not only through specially de-signed courses delivered through a variety of media, but also through completion of a Learning Portfolio of on-the-job application assign-ments, and by self-directed learning. The portfolio consisted of the fol-lowing:

- Résumé and biographical information
- Education
- Development plan and tools
- Skills transfer record and work examples
- Assessments
- Four dimensions of renewal—physical, mental, spiritual, and so-cial emotional

This holistic approach to personal and professional development be-came the foundation for learning and assessment. Anthem used an "inside-out" approach to leadership development in which the associ-ate "must be an effective individual in order to be an effective leader." In other words, it is not enough just to teach people skills. Training, management, supervision, and coaching must also help to enhance all aspects of personal and professional effectiveness in alignment with Anthem's core cultural values of Customer Focus, Commitment to Ex-cellence, Continuous Improvement and Innovation, Results with In-tegrity, and Teamwork.

Each participant prepared their own goal statements based on a competency model assessment and 360° feedback assessment. They contracted with their managers for coaching and support, tracked their progress via an online database, and were provided recognition of their achievements throughout the program.

The leadership foundation courses were based on Stephen Covey's *Seven Habits of Highly Effective People.** Additional classroom learn-ing emphasized Fundamentals of Effective Communication, Feed-back and Coaching, Creating a Great Place to Work, and Team Effectiveness.

An important element of the program was role-playing. This Level 2 activity was designed to give each participant plenty of opportunity to learn and practice each skill, as they readied themselves to apply

---

*Stephen R. Covey, *Seven Habits of Highly Effective People* (Free Press, 1990).

these skills on the job (Level 3). They also had the opportunity in their one-on-one sessions to get individual instruction, feedback, and coaching from the facilitator, HR partners, peers, and managers. Similarly, skills practice sessions allowed for mastery of new skills by modeling behaviors demonstrated during in-person and videotaped review of fellow participants. Completion criteria was provided to participants for each module and in preparation for the pretest, posttest, final roleplay, and learning transfer assessments.

TRANSFERRING LEARNING TO BEHAVIOR

Special effort was made to build a number of methods into the training from the beginning, to encourage these levels of learning transfer. They are separated into two categories, support and accountability.

Support

1. Executive and management sponsorship was critical for success. Input from all levels of management in the design and implementation of the program increased the level of the engagement and commitment to the process. This also provided a framework for measuring changes in team lead behaviors, and for coaching and encouragement during the training period. This partnership increased management's belief in the program and ownership of reinforcing the new behaviors to bring about behavior change on the job and the results expected.

2. Executives and managers were greatly involved in the actual delivery of the modules and postprogram assessment. This gave great credibility to the program in the eyes of the team leads, and helped to drive home the desired behavior changes in the hearts and minds of those senior leaders who participated. Managers were also trained in followup techniques to encourage new behaviors.

3. There is no better way to support change than to make expectations for change clear to the participants. The purpose, roles, responsibilities, specific expectations, desired outcomes, rewards, and consequences were made clear to all participants from the onset. Extensive efforts were made from the beginning to make the training enjoyable, interesting, and relevant. Feedback surveys were conducted following each module to measure impact and identify ways to improve the delivery of training and materials based on the needs of the participants.

4. Managers and team leads periodically attended training modules together. This was a powerful way to encourage and motivate all participants. This partnership carried forward beyond the actual training, which greatly increased the transfer of learning to new behaviors for *both* groups of participants.

5. Tools were provided to track and measure behavior change and success on the job. The Development Planning and Tracking online database and the Skills Transfer Action Planner, found within the learning portfolio, acted as supportive documents and methods for each participant to track their own progress. Self-supportive methodology was built into the program, rather than relying solely on external methods. Participants were also encouraged to identify their support needs with their managers and contract with them through a formal agreement. Managers could also provide feedback to team leads via the online database to recognize demonstrated skills transfer on the job. Research supports the notion that internal support and accountability are stronger than external. The success of this was evident by the fact that participants voluntarily formed their own study groups and organized their own practice sessions.

6. Results and behavior change were celebrated along the way. HR consultants acted as coaches during the sessions, and made sure positive attitudes, efforts, and the display of new behaviors at all stages of the training were recognized. A peer-awarded traveling trophy was given following monthly classroom activities to reinforce demonstrated learning and behavior change. Additionally, associates and managers could nominate team leads for a quarterly leadership excellence award for demonstrating effective application of their new skills and knowledge back on the job. An online nomination process was designed so the team lead and their manager would receive a real-time copy of the recognition submission.

7. Graduation was fun! All graduates received $500, a plaque, and a watch. Celebrations were held at major locations throughout the Midwest. The president of Anthem Midwest as well as other executives personally offered words of thanks and praise for the participants' accomplishments. Awards and trophies were given to both team leads and managers, who were viewed as role models of the program by their peers.

8. Testimonials of team leads, managers, and facilitators were taped. These were shown at the graduation and in a comprehensive video of the entire initiative to celebrate success and to provide closure.

Accountability

1. All of the aforementioned documentation served as a method of holding people accountable for change and subsequent results. Managers and facilitators used both formal and informal methods to measure progress of participants. Pre- and postassessments were administered for each module to identify levels of learning. These reports and subjective feedback from facilitators were sent to managers to aid in further coaching. Individuals needing additional development support were afforded feedback discussions, modeling and coaching. Senior leaders were given summary reports during and after training to identify specific outcomes of the program.

2. Homework assignments were an integral part of each module to ensure learning transfer outside the classroom. These work assignments were always linked to their jobs to add an element of relevance to their learning. Participants were allowed to complete these assignments while at work. A joint assignment for both team leads and managers was linked to ongoing efforts to involve associates with Great Place to Work initiatives.

3. The pre- and postsatisfaction surveys were conducted with participants to allow for real-time modifications in training methods. This also served as a way to hold the facilitators accountable for conducting the most effective workshops possible.

4. To facilitate feedback and coaching, both managers and team leads documented new behaviors that were demonstrated and observed via an online tracking system. Managers met regularly with team leads to review progress and push for application of what was learned.

5. Team leads and managers also participated in pre- and postassessments at the beginning and end of the program to share accountability for specific behavior changes based on key job competencies.

6. As mentioned under the "Support" heading, team leads developed their own accountability systems. This occurred primarily in their study groups where participants often partnered to hold themselves and each other accountable. These informal groups became the foundation for cohort teams developed for role-plays during their final assessments.

7. Participants were responsible for completing a Demonstrated Learning Folder for their final assessment. Examples included personal application of *The Seven Habits of Highly Effective People*, descriptions of development goals and accomplishments, and samples of recognized behavior change based on feedback and recognition from others. Exec-

utives reviewed the folders, asked questions, and evaluated participants on their results.

8. Another component of the final assessment involved evaluation of team leads by an executive and facilitator during role-plays conducted with their peers, to show how effectively they applied key concepts taught in the classroom.

OUTCOMES

A *Frontline Leadership Team Lead Development End-of-Program Summary* was developed in May 2004. On the front it says, "We made it!" The following was taken from that document:

- 300 team leads participated in the 2003–2004 program.
- 125 hours of classroom training per participant
- 93 percent successful program completion rate
- A postprogram talent assessment identified high-potential team leads.
- 92 percent met or exceeded participants' expectations.
- 95 percent met or exceeded managers' expectations.
- 100 percent met or exceeded directors' expectations.
- Facilitation reaction scores 4.20 out of 5.0
- Overall satisfaction 3.87 out of 5.0

THREE KEYS TO SUCCESS

We can clearly say that the following factors made the greatest impact on the program's success:

1. *Clear goals and objectives.* Significant work went into evaluating where the needs were greatest and where the program could have the greatest impact, based on the findings of an organizational analysis. By engaging key stakeholders in the process of defining the goals and objectives of the program, HR ensured that the results would be meaningful, measurable, and sustainable.

2. *High level of stakeholder engagement.* The vision was to create a foundation for continued improvement beyond the time frame of the program, to drive changes in performance and culture on an ongoing basis. It was clear from the beginning that a high degree of engagement

by all parties must be incorporated to maintain the necessary momentum and to capitalize on the program elements in the long term. The amount of time, energy, and resources needed for an extended nine-month program required it. The emphasis placed on measurements incorporated throughout the program's design ensured that HR and business sponsors could assess and adapt to the changing needs of participants. The results are indicative of the success achieved in every area that the stakeholders evaluated.

3. *Relevance to the work setting.* Shaping future behavior change requires living it. By creating a high degree of relevance on the job, through course design, work assignments, applications, and assessments, program designers produced multilevel success for participants and associates in their work areas. Through the use of recognition, and reward, the program actually created opportunities for all associates within the participating business units to observe and witness real changes in the way Anthem conducts business within work teams and in support of customers. The evaluation, recognition, and reward components became reinforcing and continue to sustain those changes going forward.

A *final note*: Many of these team leads started the Frontline Leadership Team Lead Development Program with trepidation. During review of the results and through testimonials, a significant number of these associates were noted to have greatly improved attitudes toward the company and their jobs and increased satisfaction with the program.

Indiana Institute of Technology

Sandy Bradley, Director of Operations

STRATEGIC CHALLENGE

Dr. Arthur Snyder took over as President of the Indiana Institute of Technology (Indiana Tech) in July 2003. He immediately set about to make positive changes. A major philosophy he brought in was the concept of "DIPIS," or "Does It Positively Impact Students?" Dr. Snyder insists that DIPIS goes beyond philosophy. He explains that it is all about "why we do business." He wants employees at all levels to live and breathe it by asking and answering that question whenever changes are being considered. Prior to Dr. Snyder's appointment as President, the leadership of Indiana Institute of Technology attempted to balance the academic and business aspects of the institution. Dr. Snyder believes that a deliberate shift in focus—to the major stockholders, the students—was necessary to carry the institution to the next level of excellence. Fortunately, he has received enthusiastic commitment from his staff regarding DIPIS. This case study highlights what a particular leader—Sandy Bradley—does with her direct reports to put DIPIS into practice.

TRAINING INTERVENTION

Sandy has one half-time and three full-time people reporting to her. She and her staff are in charge of operations at the Indianapolis campus. Sandy says that her initial efforts in preparing the way for operationalizing DIPIS was to pass along to her staff what DIPIS was and then to lead a discussion as to how they might go about making changes to incorporate this directive. She did this in periodic operations meetings, where she encouraged a lot of interaction and input. She said that it was challenging for them to align their work with DIPIS, since they are very task and deadline driven. Sandy states that clear, tight procedures are the key to success in operations. Therefore, the group determined that to always be able to meet students' needs (like getting their grades on time), there had to be a high degree of cross-training. Transferable skills are not only good for personal career growth, but allow for achieving deadlines when someone might be out sick.

To put DIPIS into practice, they developed standards for all skills and tasks, then trained to those procedures and standards. She continually challenged them to look at what they were doing from a student's perspective, and what effect it would have on them to miss a deadline. Sandy also helped keep the group focused on the higher vision and strategy that challenging and pleasing students was job security for all of them.

Sandy is very deliberate with her training methods. She assesses the learning styles of each of her employees and builds in visual, auditory, and hands-on learning methodology. She includes script writing and lots of practice. The specific training content is not important in this case study, but the way Sandy went about promoting the transfer of learning to behavior is.

THE TRANSFER OF LEARNING TO BEHAVIOR

Sandy makes sure that her people can talk with her about concerns and misperceptions. She behaves in ways to make herself approachable to them. She offers continual encouragement and support to her staff. Sandy believes that they must feel good about themselves if they are going to take initiative and ownership with their jobs and be willing to take risks in order to promote the DIPIS mindset.

One of the methods Sandy uses to build the confidence of her people is to get them to teach each other. Angela Snyder, one of her direct reports, is an excellent employee. In particular, Angela has exceptional computer skills. As Angela teaches the others in the department what she knows, she gains confidence and is more willing to bring forth creative ideas for doing their work more effectively. Sandy has told Angela and the others that *expectation for growth* is part of each of their jobs. Sandy helps them identify ways they want to grow, then sets up opportunities for them. Several months ago, Sandy challenged Angela to improve her presentation and public speaking skills. Although Sandy had been ready for Angela to seek speaking opportunities months ago, she sensed that Angela wasn't ready. Since she knew Angela was a good worker and had the potential to be a great one, she patiently waited until the right time. Angela is now taking classes at Indiana Tech and is working toward a degree in HR. Just the other day, Sandy sensed that Angela would benefit from a different kind of public speaking experience, so she arranged it so that Angela would be one of the employees who would have lunch with Dr. Snyder on his upcoming visit to Indianapolis. With some fear and trepidation, Angela agreed. Long story short—Angela got rave reviews for being genuine, enthusiastic, and engaging.

Sandy believes in a balance of accountability with support—and knowing when to use each. She is straightforward about expectations and when she thinks someone can do better. She continually challenges each to review their tasks, in an effort to bring about a more positive effect on the students.

Several months ago, Sandy was coaching one of her employees who did not comfortably take on the important role of "team player." Sandy approached her and said, "You are not called upon often to move outside your usual role to help your coworkers, but I need you to be ready to do so when the need arises." Seeing that her words were only partially getting through, she set up an ongoing scenario where this person was paired up with another, working side-by-side and helping each other. Unfortunately, the reluctant employee decided not to accept this directive and is now working for another institution.

OUTCOMES

Sandy's area uses a lot of measures—both numeric and nonnumeric—to gauge success. Their team regularly reviews those measures and indicators, and strives to improve them (particularly the ones that directly lead to DIPIS). Department numbers are good, and so is the morale in the department. Outcomes and impact are not always measurable. Following are comments from Angela, which demonstrate the subjective impact of a balanced approach:

Q: "How long have you been with the university, and what do you do?"

A: "About three years. I work on all of the operations in the Indianapolis area sites. That includes teacher evaluations, grades, textbooks, and a lot of other tasks that involve the smooth running of the undergraduate and graduate programs."

Q: "What methods does Sandy use to help you to apply what you have learned?"

A: "She sees and treats me as an adult. She is open with me about challenges the department faces and doesn't keep me in the dark. In a previous job, I was treated like a child—told only what I was supposed to do. She has confidence in me and knows that I can be trusted. She is also very honest. If I am doing something that may not be the best way, she will challenge me to try to improve."

Q: "Anything else about what she does?"

A: "I was scared of her at first. She told me, 'I may look intense at times, but I want you to know I am always available and willing to talk.' I found out that she meant that, and that has been very helpful for me. She also encourages my professional growth. She said she saw potential in me and said I need a degree to get to where I want to be, so I am working on that."

Q: "Do you have a career area you are interested in?"

A: "Yes, Human Resources. Not only am I taking courses with that in mind, but Sandy provides me with opportunities to learn some HR skills in my current job, such as processing new hire tasks."

Q: "I hear you went to lunch with Dr. Snyder."

A: "Yes. I was nervous about it, but approached it with confidence and actually said quite a bit. I later heard that I did a good job."

Q: "How well is this DIPIS going over?"

A: "Very well. Everyone seems to understand it and believe in it. Dr. Snyder talked a lot about it during lunch, and we all shared how we apply it."

Q: "Sandy sounds like a real caring person. Is she a soft manager?"

A: "No! She is clear about what she expects, yet finds ways of giving me feedback and suggestions without making me feel put down. She gets her point across without yelling. I think Dr. Snyder's style of leadership is being modeled by others. I see people at all leadership levels being open, supportive, respectful, and focused on our students. There is a lot of stress in my job due to the fact that we work hard, but it is great to work in a place that doesn't create fear. That's the bad kind of stress!"

Q: "What effect has all this had on you?"

A: "It has given me confidence in all areas of my life. Like last week. I went to a company to interview the HR director for my class and just walked right up to her, held out my hand to shake hers, and introduced myself. I hope an HR job opens up some day in Indianapolis, because I want to stay with Indiana Tech."

SUMMARY

Sandy uses a balance of accountability and support and strongly believes in personal and professional development as a foundation for the transfer of learning to behavior. Confidence comes from growth, and confidence leads to desired behaviors. An additional key to success that was not mentioned earlier is Sandy's belief that success starts with the right hire. Although she looks for the right mix of skills in an applicant, she looks more for the right attitude. That includes a propensity toward teamwork and a learning spirit.

Indiana Public Defender Council

SUPPLEMENT TO THE APPLICATION FOR CLE CREDIT THE PUBLIC DEFENDER TRAINING PROGRAM

Prepared by
Donald S. Murphy, J.D.
Director, Performance Improvement

STRATEGIC CHALLENGE

What Happens After Training?

The Indiana Public Defender Council (IPDC) has conducted more than one hundred Continuing Legal Education credits (CLE) programs, specifically, one-day seminars and four-day workshops. These training events transfer useful information, but most participants do not experience the permanent change in advocacy skills that they desire. After a training event, participants intend to apply all the principles they have learned, but day-to-day demands cause them to lose the focus and momentum needed to sustain change.

The problem is that most training delivery systems do not allow for enough practical application and followup to create lasting change. We have identified two critical factors:

- Knowledge gained deteriorates dramatically within a few days after the training.

- An environment that does not support new behaviors drives people back to old ways of working.

TRAINING INTERVENTION

The Solution—Improving Advocacy

The mission of the IPDC is to improve the quality of indigent defense in Indiana. Since 1976, we have been working to improve lawyer competence (knowledge, habits, and skills). Two years ago, IPDC designed a professional development program for public defenders. It's a guided effort over time to integrate the knowledge, habits, and skills of effective criminal defense lawyers. The objectives of the program are twofold:

- Increase the effectiveness and performance capability of public defenders.
- Encourage public defenders to be responsible for their professional development.

We developed a sixteen-week coaching program with assistance from Indiana University Professor Thomas Schwen. Professor Schwen has extensive experience in designing adult education programs that foster problem-solving and peer-based learning. Our program helps public defenders through one-on-one coaching with skilled criminal defense lawyers. Participants apply lawyer competencies in actual criminal cases. The program also raises awareness of ethical dilemmas faced by all criminal defense lawyers.

Why This Approach?

Experts in adult education have found that experiential training— training that occurs in the work environment—is the most effective way to acquire and sustain skills. Also, adults have an increased commitment to professional development when they are involved in the design of their learning experiences.

In our program, training is not an event; it's a process. The lawyer and the coach identify performance barriers, customize developmental plans, and apply new behaviors in actual criminal cases. This one-on-one approach fosters candid discussions about the lawyer's inadequacies and weaknesses. In addition, the personalized approach helps integrate core knowledge, skills, and abilities into the lawyer's individual style. Periodic consultation and support continues after formal completion of the program.

Summary of Program Features

Sponsoring Agency

- IPDC, a state agency whose mission is to improve the quality of indigent defense
- IPDC, an approved CLE sponsor

Trainees

- Salaried and contract public defenders or assigned counsel
- Participate free of charge

Trainers

- Independent contractors of IPDC
- No pecuniary relationship with trainee or trainee's employer
- Criminal defense lawyers with substantial teaching experience

Adult Learning Principles

- Program uses real cases of trainee, not simulated exercises.
- 1:1 trainer to trainee relationship
- Between sessions, students have time to practice and form new habits.
- Sixteen-week program requiring a minimum of two hours per week

Requirements to Enroll

- Both trainees and trainers must commit a minimum of two hours per week for training.
- Neither trainees nor trainers can bill clients for the time spent in training.

Accountability

- Trainers submit claim vouchers that are audited by IPDC.
- Claim vouchers are subject to audits by the State of Indiana auditor's office.
- Trainers document activities completed at each session.
- Practical—each week you know your coach is going to ask what you did.

Evaluation

- Trainees evaluate effectiveness of the program and effectiveness of the trainers.
- IPDC conducts focus groups with trainees to continually improve program.
- Curriculum review with trainers.

- Trainers prepare written progress reports for trainees.
- Measure changes in on-the-job behavior.

Written Materials

- Two three-ring binders with more than 200 pages of checklists, articles, and practice aids in the following subjects: Assessing Your Strengths and Weaknesses; Competencies of Criminal Defense Lawyers; Criminal Defense Trial Case Review; Monitor Progress and Action Plans; Brainstorming; Initial Case Preparation; Investigation; Pretrial Motions and Hearings; Trial Preparation; *Voir Dire*; Opening Statement; Cross Examination; Direct Examination; Exhibits; Indiana Rules of Evidence; Closing Argument; Instructions; Post Verdict and Sentencing.*

OUTCOMES

Program Evaluation by Graduates

Figure 5.

---

*This entire case study was designed with the intention to transfer learning to behavior.

Figure 6.

**Because of the coaching program,
my skills have improved in:**

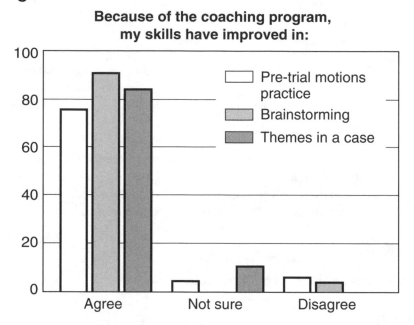

Figure 7.

**Because of the coaching program,
my skills have improved in:**

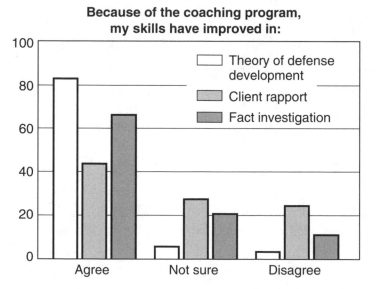

Figure 8.

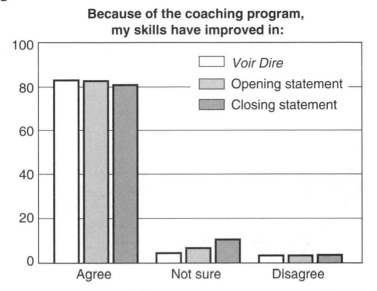

**Because of the coaching program,
my skills have improved in:**

KEYS TO SUCCESS*

- **Knowledge**. Information delivered in small increments over time. Principles and concepts presented are relevant and applicable to personal needs of each participant.

- **Application**. Help trainees apply principles and concepts to their unique situations. Learning occurs step by applied step.

- **Accountability**. Strong relationship of personal accountability. Objectives established, goals set, and commitments are made and followed up on.

- **Motivation**. Personal coaching produces drive to learn and change as participants experience satisfying exchanges with coaches. As they apply principles and experience benefits of new behaviors, motivation shifts from external to internal.

- **Time**. To internalize concepts and make lasting changes. Gives people time to think about concepts, practice principles, get feedback, make adjustments, overcome stumbling blocks, and try again.

---

*Taken from an S. Covey Personal Coaching flyer.

First Indiana Bank

COMMERCIAL OPERATIONS

David Drake, Manager
Kelly Trips, Administrator

STRATEGIC CHALLENGE

The 2003 strategic directive for Dave Drake's department, Commercial Banking Operations, was straightforward: provide internal partners with accurate, timely, and efficient service so that sales associates can serve external customers as trusted advisors and facilitate a First Indiana Experience for them. Although there was nothing new in that challenge, it was up to Dave to figure out how to enhance it.

TRAINING AND COACHING INTERVENTION

The following is taken from interviews with Dave and with one of his team leads, Kelly Trips. Dave's first task was to assess how well his area measured and reported key data. They had a monthly balanced scorecard, but most of the internal quality measures routinely came in as 99.9 percent satisfactory. Neither he nor Kelly believed that those Customer Impact Error numbers were accurate because they knew that errors in accuracy did occur, and turn-around times for returning phone calls to customers were not perfect (or even 99.9 percent). Dave asked Kelly to attend one of Jim Kirkpatrick's Balanced Scorecard classes to see what they could learn. The question arises, "Why didn't Dave himself go, since he was ultimately responsible for the numbers and his department's service?" The answer is (1) Dave had attended a previous class, and (2) he believes that his managers and supervisors must be the ones to make prudent improvements, since they are closest to the service processes.

Dave expects each of his direct reports to initiate what he calls self-development projects (SDPs), which not only facilitate professional growth but also make great contributions to the organization. Dave states, "Involvement creates ownership. I will free them up from other responsibilities to carry out their projects, and will clear away barriers as best I can. I also make myself available for regular progress meetings and coaching, but they are the ones driving the projects." Dave is a coach on and off the job. He coaches his children's sports teams and uses many of those same coaching methods on the job. He believes in strong direction, but knows "my players must actually play the game. I cannot do it for them, but I can equip them to play [do] their best."

One of Kelly's SDPs was to improve the department's balanced scorecard, and ultimately service to internal and external customers. The direct and indirect training Kelly received to attack and successfully complete came in three forms:

- Jim's Balance Scorecard class
- First Indiana University's Coaching class that Dave took
- Dave's on-the-job training and coaching

Kelly's Comments: I was aware that the numbers on our BSC were not entirely accurate. Even though I work in operations, I know that if we don't provide exceptional service to our customers, they will leave, and then what's the point? There is too much competition out there for us to offer less than the best in products and service. I take pride in my job. If we don't accurately report what we are doing, why do it? I am glad I was assigned this project, because I believed I could make it better.

TRANSFERRING LEARNING TO BEHAVIOR

Dave utilizes a balance of both *accountability* and *support* to get the most out of his direct reports. Let's look at them one at a time.

Accountability

1. Dave gives clear expectations and checks for understanding. He made sure that Kelly knew what outcomes he wanted to see as a result of her work with their balanced scorecard.

2. He met with Kelly on a weekly basis to discuss project milestones that Kelly had set. She was responsible for bringing to Dave progress, barriers, and projected next steps. Dave notes that he holds her to task and strongly challenges unmet commitments (which, by the way, Kelly didn't have).

3. Dave asked and received a commitment from Kelly for her to share final results with Marni, First Indiana Bank's chairman. *This is a big one!* Both Dave and Kelly later reported that they could not have

come up with a better way of motivating Kelly to do her very best with her project. Kelly said, "I am strongly motivated from within myself always to do a good job, but having the opportunity to present our work to Marni was a very strong motivator, and certainly helped hold me accountable."

Support

Dave, by his own admission, is not exactly a "touchy-feely" guy. "Warm fuzzy" is not his approach, though he still offers a lot when it comes to supporting his people. Kelly states that his belief in her is all the support she needs. Dave formally and informally recognizes accomplishments along the way, and routinely discusses career aspirations with his direct reports, which is strongly supportive and motivating. Finally, Dave arranged for Kelly and her team to get recognition from others (e.g., Marni and Jim). He shies away from drawing attention to himself, expertly deflecting it to his people.

Kelly met with her team regularly to explore and decide on improved Customer Impact Error measures and how to report them. She included discussions with sales leaders to ensure that the measures they selected were truly the ones customers cared about the most. Finally, they brainstormed and settled on methods for more accurate measurement.

Kelly's Comments: "Dave allows us to be creative and lets us run with new ideas. He has an open-door policy, yet never lets us get too far afield by offering constant followup. He encourages us to motivate and involve our entire team in the planning and executing of these projects. He also reviews our balanced scorecard in our monthly meetings to demonstrate its importance and his support of it."

OUTCOMES

Commercial Operations now has improved, more relevant Customer Impact Errors on their balanced scorecard. They can quickly recognize a pattern of a certain type of error and correct it. The whole team now takes pride in watching for and improving these measures, and in seeing how improved service led to a significant increase in Quarter 2, 2004, customer loyalty and sales.

Other positive outcomes included improved morale, stronger "bench strength" and teamwork, and improved relationships with in-

ternal partners. Finally, Kelly gained new skills in the area of presentations and project management.

The fundamental key to success is this: Dave is *development-minded*
and *training-minded*. Don't we wish all of our line-of-business managers
were?

Chapter 11

Taking Action

None of this is of much value unless you do something with it. Transferring *your* learning to behavior is now up to you. Here are a few suggestions as you consider what to do next.

1. Sit back and consider what is the vision for performance enhancement in your organization. Spell it out from as high a level as you can. Consult others if you are unsure. If it is weak or nonexistent, spend some time developing what you think it should be. See if you can get some understanding and buy-in from executives.

2. Review Chapters 3 through 8 and identify elements to be addressed or improved to accomplish the vision. Look for dysfunctional and missing elements as well as barriers to success.

3. Review Chapters 3 through 8 and identify what your organization is good at.

4. Review the case studies for approaches and methods that you can adopt or modify to bring performance enhancement to your organization.

5. Put these first four steps together into an action plan. Get input from others. Do a good job of preparing it in the form of a business plan. Present it to senior executives, gain their enthusiastic approval (one hopes), and get to it.

TOP TEN MISTAKES

We thought it might be helpful to include the top ten mistakes leaders make when trying to transfer learning to behavior. Watch out for them as you develop and implement your action plan.

Number 10: Not linking and aligning incentives to desired behavior and subsequent results.

Number 9: Trying to do too much and not focusing efforts on mission critical behavior.

Number 8: Having the wrong kind of leaders, or the right kind in the wrong positions.

Number 7: Not providing adequate technology and system support.

Number 6: Not providing a balance of accountability and support.

Number 5: Not providing clear direction—vision, strategy, and expectations.

Number 4: Promoting a culture of employees who are discouraged from learning.

Number 3: Not developing action plans from a business consulting approach.

Number 2: Not following up and following through.

Number 1: Not eliciting buy-in and involvement from executives.

This past July, I (Jim) was in Kuala Lumpur, Malaysia, attending and speaking at a conference called the *2004 Asia HRD Congress* put on by Specialist Management Resources (SMR). On the first day, I sat in on a workshop led by the founder and president of SMR, Dr. R. Palan. The workshop was on creativity. Dr. Palan not only spoke about creativity, he demonstrated it throughout his workshop. At the beginning, for instance, he had each participant—probably 120 of us—blow up a balloon and write an important aspect of creativity on it with a marker. I must say that I am not too fond of blowing up balloons because I don't like it when they pop.

After that ice-breaking exercise, people tossed their balloons on the floor. Every once in awhile, during the rest of the workshop a balloon would burst. No matter how hard I tried not to, I jumped each time. Another interesting phenomenon was happening at the same time. We were all sitting at tables of about six. There were about ten big balloons ready to pop, near mine. For some reason, they all seemed to be at my feet. It was very hard for me to concentrate on what Dr. Palan was saying, as I knew that any second, one of them would go. Since I couldn't just sit there and wait for that to happen, I started nudging them away with my feet. There must have been a current of air or something in the room because no matter how far I nudged them, they would always come back to me. I finally resorted to kicking them and, unfortunately, made quite a spectacle of myself. Even that didn't work. They seemed to have legs and would slowly crawl along the floor until they were surrounding me again. There was one in particular—a huge green one with a big smiley face drawn on it—that seemed the most eager for my company.

Consider the balloons as you think back on the case studies that you just read. You will note some strong trends, including strategic focus, executive involvement, and good communication. You will also note two or three particularly relevant points that beckon to you like the big green smiley face balloon. Pay attention to those issues. Discuss them with others and make a commitment to address them as soon as possible, as you help move your organization toward higher successes. It may also save you a big bang down the road.

Where to Find More Information

Corporate University Enterprise at www.cuenterprise.com

Robert Brinkerhoff's model for evaluating training at
www.advantageperformance.com

Jack Phillips' model for evaluating training at
www.franklincovey.com/jackphillips/roi.html

Knowledge Advisors training evaluation software at
www.knowledgeadvisors.com

Kirkpatrick Consulting at www.donaldkirkpatrick.com

Index

About the Authors

Don and Jim are coauthors, and much more besides. As father and son, their favorite activity together is fishing, whether in the meandering trout streams of southwestern Wisconsin or the remote lakes of Canada. They also enjoy traveling with other members of their families, playing tennis (Don gives Jim lessons), croquette (Jim gives Don lessons), or golf (they both need lessons from someone else). They also work together, frequently taking advantage of organizations or groups that want a more customized session on training, evaluation, and performance. Their most popular venture is a three-tier Kirkpatrick Certification Program in the four levels. As individuals . . .

Donald L. Kirkpatrick is a Professor Emeritus, University of Wisconsin, and a widely respected teacher, author, and consultant. He has over thirty years of experience as professor of management at the University of Wisconsin and has held professional training and human resource positions with International Minerals and Chemical Corporation and Bendix Corporation. He is the author of eight management inventories and six books: *Evaluating Training Programs: The Four Lev-*

els, *How to Manage Change Effectively*, *How to Improve Performance Through Appraisal and Coaching*, *How to Train and Develop Supervisors*, *How to Plan and Conduct Productive Business Meetings*, and *No-Nonsense Communication*. He has received the Best Book of the Year award from the Society for Human Resource Management. Don is past president of the American Society for Training and Development (ASTD) and is best known for developing the internationally accepted four-level approach for evaluating training programs. In 1997, he was introduced into *TRAINING* magazine's Hall of Fame, and in 2004 received the Lifetime Achievement award from ASTD. He received his BBA, MBA, and PhD degrees from the University of Wisconsin. He lives in Pewaukee, Wisconsin, and is a senior elder at Elmbrook Church and an active member of Gideons International.

James D. Kirkpatrick has worked in the field of organizational development for over fifteen years. He recently teamed with Corporate University Enterprise, Inc. in a leadership and senior consulting role to orchestrate and launch the Kirkpatrick Four Level Evaluation Certification Program and a robust approach to scorecarding and evaluation practice to support learning organizations through their corporate universities. Jim considers his expertise with balanced scorecards, evaluation, and transferring learning to behavior as his greatest assets. He is a former Vice President and Director of First Indiana Bank's corporate university, First Indiana University. He was responsible for First Indiana's balanced scorecard management system, leadership development, training, and the Career Development Program.

Jim has also worked as a management consultant in the fields of healthcare, education, finance, manufacturing, not-for-profits, and government. He has designed and facilitated workshops and consulted in a number of U.S. cities, as well as in Canada, Europe, Colombia, Australia, India, and Malaysia. He also has relevant experience as a career consultant and clinical psychologist.

Jim currently serves on the Advisory Board for the American Red Cross and is an adjunct professor in the Indiana Institute of Technology's MBA program. Jim has bachelor's and master's degrees from the University of Wisconsin, and a PhD in Counseling Psychology from Indiana State University. He is active in ASTD national and is cofounder of the Indianapolis Downtown Organizational Development Network.

Evaluating Training Programs
The Four Levels, Third Edition

Donald L. Kirkpatrick and James D. Kirkpatrick

In 1959 Donald Kirkpatrick developed a four-level model for evaluating training programs. Since then, the "Kirkpatrick Model" has become the most widely used approach to training evaluation in the corporate, government, and academic worlds.

Evaluating Training Programs provided the first comprehensive guide to Kirkpatrick's Four Level Model, along with detailed case studies of how the model is being used successfully in a wide range of programs and institutions.

In the third edition of this classic bestseller, Kirkpatrick offers new forms and procedures for evaluating at all levels and several additional chapters about using balanced scorecards and "Managing Change Effectively." He also includes twelve new case studies from organizations that have been evaluated using one or more of the four levels-Caterpillar, Defense Acquisition University, Microsoft, IBM, Toyota, Noxtel, The Regence Group, Denison University, and Pollack Learning Alliance.

Hardcover, 288 pages
ISBN 978-1-57675-348-4
Item #93484-415 $39.95

Berrett-Koehler Publishers
PO Box 565, Williston, VT 05495-9900
Call toll-free! **800-929-2929** 7 am-9 pm EST

Or fax your order to 1-802-864-7626
For fastest service order online: **www.bkconnection.com**